907110

THE RACE QUESTION AND MODERN THOUGHT

AF327228

TRINITY UNIVERSITY LIBRARIES

In the same series

The Catholic Church and the Race Question,
        by the Rev. Yves M.-J. Congar, O.P.
Jewish Thought as a Factor in Civilization,
        by Léon Roth
The Ecumenical Movement, the Churches and the Race Problem,
        by Dr. W. A. Visser't Hooft

In the series *The Race Question in Modern Science*

Race and Culture,
        by Michel Leiris
Race and Psychology,
        by Otto Klineberg
Race and Biology,
        by L. C. Dunn
Racial Myths,
        by Juan Comas
The Roots of Prejudice,
        by Arnold M. Rose
Race and History,
        by Claude Lévi-Strauss
Race and Society,
        by Kenneth L. Little
The Significance of Racial Differences,
        by G. M. Morant
Race Mixture,
        by Harry L. Shapiro

The Race Concept : Results of an Inquiry

BUDDHISM AND THE RACE QUESTION

by

G. P. MALALASEKERA

*Dean of the Faculty of Oriental Studies
and Professor of Pali and Buddhist Civilization,
University of Ceylon*

and

K. N. JAYATILLEKE

*Lecturer in Philosophy,
University of Ceylon*

UNESCO

*Published in 1958 by the United Nations
Educational, Scientific and Cultural Organization,
19 Avenue Kléber, Paris-16e
Printed by Firmin-Didot et Cie*

© Unesco 1958
Printed in France
SS. 57 IX. 5A

The series in which Buddhism and the Race Question *is appearing consists of publications designed to give a brief outline of the attitude of the main religious and philosophical systems to the problems created by the diversity of human types and the inequalities in treatment which it has served to excuse. The present booklet follows those which have described the views of Catholicism, Protestantism and Judaism on this subject. Then will come further studies, summarizing the relevant theories or doctrines of other religions.*

Buddhist thinkers have concentrated on the barriers erected between castes in Indian society, rather than on the relations between different ethnic groups. Very many works have been devoted to this problem, which is still as topical as ever; and the task of bringing out the main trends and selecting the most significant passages from the whole of this vast literature has taxed the two authors' great erudition to the full. The reason why Mr. Malalasekera and Mr. Jayatilleke have confined themselves to this particular aspect of the subject is that, like many historians and sociologists, they attribute the origin of the caste system, at least in large measure, to the 'racism' of the Indo-European invaders of India. This theory is still widely accepted though it is not subscribed to by all experts. It has been suggested that the attribution of such 'pride of race' to the ancient Aryans might simply be a projection, into prehistoric times, of attitudes which are peculiar to contemporary society and have emerged only comparatively recently. Another theory put forward is that the Sanskrit word varna, *which means 'colour' as well as 'caste', might refer to a symbolic system and not to a social hierarchy based on the colour of men's skins. Be this as it may, Indian society was already very mixed at the time when the caste system took final shape, and it was not until after the fusion of the indigenous with the Indo-European peoples that the restrictions on marriage between members of different castes became entirely hard and fast.*

The authors of this booklet rightly stress the close analogy between the inequalities created by the caste system and those existing, in various countries, between different racial groups. The resemblance is particularly striking when it comes to the behaviour of those who claim superiority on the strength of membership of a privileged caste, the colour of their skin, or even the type of their hair. Nevertheless, Mr. Malalasekera and Mr. Jayatilleke are fully aware that parallels drawn between the position of inferior castes and that of certain ethnic minorities may be misleading, and that they concern psychological attitudes rather than actual conditions.

The present authors repeatedly stress the close similarity between Buddhist thought and the findings of modern science. There is no doubt that Buddhism, in proclaiming the one-ness of the human species, is in line with modern biological theory; but such comparisons should not blind us to the fact that the lessons of human brotherhood preached by a philosophy thousands of years old derive from searchings quite other than those underlying present-day laboratory work. The really important points are the profoundly 'modern' character of Buddhist thought, —though it is more than two thousand years old—and the lessons in tolerance which it has imparted to men all over the world.

In issuing this study on a subject which has exercised Buddhist thinkers since the earliest times, Unesco has been simply concerned to publicize various opinions on the differences dividing groups of human beings. The Organization adopts no position in the debates between philosophers and scholars. Its one and only aim is to bring these debates to the knowledge of the general public, and to promote a free exchange of views on a question of prime importance.

All references to Pali texts are to the editions of the Pali Text Society (London). The standard abbreviations are used, namely:

    D = Digha Nikaya
    M = Majjhima Nikaya
    S = Samyutta Nikaya
    A = Anguttara Nikaya
    J = Jataka
   Sn = Sutta Nipata

INTRODUCTION

This pamphlet proposes to give in outline the Buddhist attitude to the problem of race and related questions. It would appear that the Unesco booklets on this subject not only cover the ground from their respective fields of study such as biology, psychology, history, anthropology and sociology, but seek also to provide a forum for expressing the attitude of the world's main religions and philosophies to this question. In this introduction we shall seek to clarify the relation of Buddhism to science, religion and philosophy in general, to bring out the significance of Buddhist statements on this subject, and also to bring into better focus the distinctive character of the Buddhist contribution towards understanding and resolving this problem.

It may be stated at the outset that the authors assume that the reader has an elementary background knowledge of the history of Buddhism as a religion, and no attempt will therefore be made to provide a biographical sketch of the Founder or to give an account of his doctrines or their history where this has no bearing on the problem. It may, however, be said that a movement which spread into many countries and has lasted two thousand five hundred years has undoubtedly undergone many ramifications, and some may question the prudence and propriety of making general statements about Buddhism which are authoritative, or applicable alike to all phases of Buddhist thought and activity. At first sight there may appear to be little in common between say, the mysticism of Tibetan Buddhism and the rational temper of the Ceylon tradition or again, the doctrines of salvation through personal effort as advocated in the southern school of Buddhism (Theravāda) as opposed to the salvation through faith in the Buddha of Infinite Splendour (Amitābha) as taught in some of the Mahāyāna schools.

But to make a clear-cut distinction between the doctrines of the Elders (Theravāda), as the southern school is called, and the Greater Vehicle (Mahāyāna) or the northern school is to miss the essential similarity or rather the basic identity of the core of doctrine that is common to both, in spite of the apparent differences in some of the outward trappings and the symbolic mythology of the different schools. To take just one point—and an important point—in illustration, the central doctrine of the Four Truths, for instance, is common to both traditions. In both these traditions it is taught that the starting point of religion is man's realization of his sense of insecurity in a changing universe in which he is subjected to physical pain and psychological suffering accompanied by the uncertainties of existence and of the hereafter. The cause of this is traced to our own ignorance and the desires which are operative within us—the desire for sense-gratification and the desire for selfish existence which alternates with the desire for annihilation. It is said to be the operation of these desires at the deepest level of the mind which is responsible for the conflicts causing that mental ill-health which, according to the texts, we ceaselessly suffer from till we attain perfection. Part of our ignorance is our ignorance both of the fact of the Blissful Infinitude of Nirvana as well as of the mode of attaining it—the Eightfold Path comprising the right philosophy of life, right aspirations, right speech, right actions, right mode of livelihood, right effort, right awareness and right tranquillity of mind terminating in the attainment of wisdom and salvation—a path which is characterized by the development of the moral nature, intelligence and the intuitive spiritual insight of the individual. It is significant that these Four Truths—as they are popularly called—which provide a diagnosis and remedy, or the causes and cure, for man's unrest in a strange world in which he lives and moves, and constitutes the central teaching of Buddhism are frequently mentioned in the texts of both schools and form the general background or the starting point of the attitude of Buddhism to most problems.

Another misconception that needs to be removed from the mind of the reader is that these two great schools split the Buddhist world into two hostile camps which opposed and persecuted each other. On the contrary, there was contact and mutual exchange of views between them, and history records the fact that members of the two schools were sometimes found in the precincts of the same monastery. This spirit is reflected still today, when at the international conferences organized by the World Fellowship of Buddhists, the members of both schools from many lands meet in complete harmony in spite of the differences in their views.

The essential difference between the two schools seems to be that while the Mahāyāna school gives a less orthodox and more picturesque interpretation of the teachings and practices and is prepared to adapt and accommodate them to suit the needs of the masses, the Theravāda school is more conservative and orthodox and tries to retain the early teaching and practices to the very letter. The origin of the two schools can possibly be traced to the separation that took place about a hundred years after the death of the Buddha (i.e., *circa* 383 B.C.) at the Second Council where there was a debate as to what were the minor rules of the Order of Monks. It had been decreed by the Buddha that after his demise the minor rules of conduct could be changed, presumably to suit the changing social and historical contexts, but a serious difference of opinion emerged at the discussion as to what these minor rules were. As no agreement where to draw the line seemed to be possible, the more orthodox Elders decided to keep all the rules and adhere to them. Whereupon the others, who were possibly more liberal and appear to have been in the majority, seceded and holding their own Council proceeded to make their own innovations. But this separation of the liberal and the orthodox does not seem to have affected the essential content of the doctrine, so that on most matters the attitude of the two schools would be fundamentally the same. In discussing the problems touching race it will therefore not be necessary—nor indeed possible—to distinguish between two different viewpoints with regard to the two schools.

We shall now proceed to give in brief outline the relation of Buddhism to science, religion and philosophy. This may give some indication how the statements of Buddhism would fall in line with or differ from the standpoints adopted in the various pamphlets of this series written from the specific points of view of the different sciences as well as of the other religions and philosophies.

BUDDHISM AND SCIENCE

Although most people are acquainted with Buddhism as a religion and would therefore be inclined to distinguish its doctrines from the outlook, methodology and findings of the sciences, in fact Early Buddhism can be stated in the form of a scientific theory which each individual who wishes to

11

test it out is to verify for himself. We find in Early Buddhism passages which can only find their parallel in the modern scientific outlook. For instance, the Buddha in one place tells a questioner: 'You have raised a doubt in a situation in which you ought to suspend your judgement. Do not accept anything because it is rumoured so, because it is the traditional belief, because the majority hold it, because it is found in the scriptures, because it is a product of metaphysical argument and speculation, because of a superficial investigation of facts, because it conforms with one's inclinations, because it is authoritative or because of the prestige value of your teacher.'

Far from being detrimental, this scientific outlook was considered to be essential for the moral and spiritual development of man. The sincerity and frankness on which a truly religious life should be grounded demanded healthy criticism and continual self-examination, and the importance of such an outlook is nowhere so well emphasized as in the following exhortation: 'If anyone', says the Buddha, 'were to speak ill of me, my doctrine or my Order of Monks, do not bear any ill-will towards him, be upset or perturbed at heart, for if you were to be so, it would only cause you harm. If on the other hand anyone were to speak well of me, my doctrine and my Order of Monks do not be overjoyed, thrilled or elated at heart, for if so it will only be an obstacle in your way of forming a correct judgement as to whether the qualities praised in us are real and actually found in us.' Even his own teaching was no exception, and Buddha did not demand a blind faith or allegiance for it: 'One must not', he is reported to have said, 'accept my Dhamma (teaching) from reverence, but must first try it as gold is tried by fire.'

This outlook goes with a causal conception of the universe. 'The Tathāgata (i.e., Buddha) speaks only of the causes of events that arise from causes.' There is even a mention of the two principles of causal determination. The events in the universe are such that 'whenever an occurrence A is found or comes into being, an occurrence B is found or comes into being and whenever an occurrence A is not found or does not come into being an occurrence B is not found or does not come into being'; and it is under such conditions that A and B are considered to be causally related. All events are thus said to be causally related and in the universe there operate 'physical laws, biological laws, psychological laws as well as moral and spiritual laws'.

12

Rebirth—or the continuity of individuality by means of which the processes of birth and organic growth are followed by decay and death, which in turn gives rise to renewed existence through the dynamic persistence of one's unconscious mental processes—is an exemplification of the law of causation. Another causal law is that of karma, according to which morally good acts are followed by pleasant consequences and morally evil acts by unpleasant consequences for the individual. Then again—while the Upanishads posited a soul (ātman) or an unverifiable entity to account for both rebirth and karma, arguing that it was an unchanging substratum common to the different lives (of the same individual) as well as the agent and enjoyer of good and evil actions and their reactions—Buddhism does away with such unverifiable entities as meaningless concepts and gives instead a more detailed account of the causally inter-related phenomena involved in rebirth and karma in order to account for them.

The relation between the Buddha and the moral and spiritual laws embodied in his teaching is again analogous to the relation between a scientist and a valid theory that he discovers. The Buddha merely discovers and proclaims these facts of existence or 'things as they really are', and it is up to us to put forth effort and realize these things for ourselves by following 'the mode of genetical reflection' of looking for causes and their effects. It is this form of scrutiny and self-analysis which constitutes the practical application of Buddhism to our daily lives, in which our critical faculties should play as important a part as our faith in moral and spiritual values.

The Dhamma (i.e., the teaching of the Buddha), however, differs from a scientific hypothesis in two respects. First, it is not considered to be in need of further modifications in the light of experience as is the case with a scientific hypothesis, though this does not mean that the same truth cannot be stated with greater or lesser detail or clarity. The Buddha considered his disciples, both male and female, as carrying on the good work that he inaugurated and on several occasions showed his appreciation and recognition of the value of detailed expositions of doctrines given by his disciples when these same doctrines had received only a more concise statement at his own hands. Secondly, the verification of a scientific hypothesis (in a natural science) would be in the light of sense-experience, while the verification of the ultimate truths of Buddhism would involve a development through the meditative culture of the mind of such latent faculties in us as telepathy, clairvoyance, clairaudience, retro-cognition and insight into our inner mental processes. Except for these two distinctions that need to be made, the analogy between Buddhism as a verifiable theory about the nature and destiny of man in the universe and a scientific hypothesis is almost complete.

The moral that we draw from all this for the problem under discussion is that Buddhism welcomes wholeheartedly the enlightenment that science can offer us by giving as objective an account as possible of the facts of race and racism. In fact, Buddhism would go so far as to say that it is only by such an informed objective study and not by the propagation of myths that we can hope to combat racial prejudice. But at the same time it would hold that the roots of prejudice are too deep-seated within us to be easily removed by merely giving our intellectual assent to the findings of the scientists, for the removal of these prejudices would require a careful and sustained self-examination which requires us to watch our thoughts and actions in our relations with our fellow-men. It is only when we can see and remove from our psychological nature and social environment the factors causing racial prejudice and discrimination that we can hope to succeed in solving this problem.

BUDDHISM AND RELIGION

A word of explanation is, perhaps, necessary as to the sense in which Buddhism is a religion. Otherwise, the statements of Buddhism are likely to be misunderstood as those of a theological tradition or a revelation of a divinely inspired prophet or teacher mediating between God and man. The sense of the English word 'religion' is so bound up with faith, worship and humility before a Personal God regarded as the author of our being, that some scholars who have not found these elements in Early Buddhism have questioned the propriety of calling Buddhism a religion.

The word used for religion in Buddhism is *brahma-cariya* which may be translated as 'the ideal life', but it is a word used with a very wide connotation to cover any way of life which anyone may consider to be the ideal as a consequence of his holding a certain set of beliefs about the nature and destiny of man in the universe. Using the term religion

14

(*brahma-cariya*) in this sense in one of the *suttas*,[1] Ananda, one of the immediate disciples of the Buddha, distinguishes the sense in which Buddhism is a religion by showing how it differs from other religions. A very brief resumé of the substance of this *sutta* may clarify the sense in which Buddhism is a religion.

In it Ananda distinguishes Buddhism from four false and four unsatisfactory types of religion, and goes on to define the distinctive character of Buddhism. The first of the four false types is any religion which denies survival and holds that man is composed entirely of material elements which disintegrate at death. The second is any religion which denies moral values. The third is any religion which denies causation and holds that 'people are miraculously saved or doomed'. The fourth type of false religion is any religion which denies free will and teaches that everything including salvation is strictly determined.

It is worth noting that the Buddhist theory of causation steers clear on the one hand from Indeterminism (*adhicca-samuppanna-vāda*), which holds that events arise unrelated to the past, and on the other hand from Strict Determinism. Such causation is said to be compatible with free will, defined as the capacity of the individual or the factor of human effort, which can within limits control or direct the operative forces of the past and present in order to make the future different from what it would otherwise have been. Strict Determinism is of two kinds. One is Natural Determinism (*sabhāva-vāda*) which holds that the present and future is a working out of the past and is therefore unalterable. The other is Theistic Determinism (*issara-nimmāna-vāda*) which holds that everything that takes place is predetermined by the will or fiat of a Personal God. In combating both these forms of determinism Buddhism holds that man is master of his fate and can by the exercise of his efforts alter the face of nature as well as his own inner nature by understanding and controlling the forces at play or the causal sequences at work. In combating the second, namely that everything happens under the guidance or the will of God, Buddhism is under no compunction to justify all that has happened merely because it has happened or to hold that all the evil perpetrated in the past was necessary in the best of all possible worlds.

---

1. Sandaka Sutta, Majjhima Nikaya; *suttas* are sermons or discourses of the Buddha or his disciples recorded in the Canonical texts.

The moral is clear. The problems of race and racism are neither inevitable nor imposed on us by the hand of God. Given the will, they can and must be solved by humans if they wish to survive as a peaceful and progressive human community.

The four types of unsatisfactory but not necessarily false religions are, first, any religion which ascribes omniscience to its teacher in the sense that he knows everything all the time. Omniscience in this sense was denied by the Buddha. The second type is any religion based on a revelational tradition, the reason being that a revelational claim may be either true or false, since the validity of a claim to revelation can only be ascertained by criteria other than that of the claim to revelation. For this reason it is very necessary that Buddhism should not be understood as a revelational religion and the sayings of the Buddha should not be considered as special revelations given to him and denied to others. As this *sutta* goes on to say, the truths of Buddhism are considered to have been verified by the Buddha and hundreds of his disciples and it is as a verifiable theory the truth or falsity of which each person can test for himself or herself that Buddhism invites others to practise this religion. Of course, verification is not merely in the light of sense experience but includes the experience of the special insights which are considered to be within the power of man to develop. In this sense the statements of Buddhism are not dogmatic utterances to be accepted on faith or faith alone. The doctrine of rebirth for instance, which to most moderns may appear to be a dogma, is considered to be verifiable by developing in us the faculty of retro-cognition. Even the textual statements are not to be taken dogmatically as the word of the Buddha, as the texts themselves state that a comparison of texts should be made to determine their authenticity.

The third type of unsatisfactory religion is one based purely on 'logical reasoning and metaphysical speculation', for here again the reasoning may be either true or false. As Buddhism is distinguished from this kind of religion it is incorrect, as is sometimes done, to call it a Pure Rationalism, or an attempt on the part of the human mind to unravel the mysteries of the universe by a process of pure reasoning. Logic can help us to evolve self-consistent systems of thought, but they need not be true of reality and there could be many such systems which are self-consistent within themselves but mutually contradict each other. The last type of unsatisfactory religion is any religion which is inconsistent, but consistency alone, as we see from the above, is no guarantee of truth. The consistency that Buddhism urges is the consistency of objective fact and not of a subjective system which may also be self-consistent.

Buddhism is thus a religion in the sense that it is a way of life following from the acceptance of a certain set of propositions which are considered to represent the facts of existence pertaining to the life and destiny of man in the universe. These propositions are also held to be true in the sense that they can be verified and discovered to be true by people who wish to do so, though verification is not merely in the light of sense experience but includes valid experiences which, it is considered, are within the capacity of the human mind to develop. The Buddha merely discovered and proclaimed these truths and since it is within the power of each one of us to re-discover them ourselves under the guidance that he has given, his was not a special revelation denied to others. On the other hand his doctrines are not the product of the mere reasoning of the human intellect, since the awakening within the mind of the faculties of extra-sensory perception makes the mind 'more than human' (*uttari-manussa-dhamma*).

BUDDHISM AND PHILOSOPHY

As it is sometimes said that Buddhism is not a religion but a philosophy, and as it appears to be the intention of Unesco 'to state the attitude of the world's main philosophical systems towards the diversity of human types',[1] it will not be out of place to make a brief statement as to where Buddhism stands in this respect.

The scientific temper of Early Buddhism naturally resulted in the adoption of a positivistic attitude to metaphysics. Inquiry into matters which are beyond the limits of human experience—such as the investigation of the origin and extent of the universe or the nature of noumenal existence—is discarded as being intellectually stultifying and morally fruitless. Speculation on matters which fall within the field of possible experience are not considered to be entirely valueless, but they are of little account when compared with personal verification and realization of the facts of existence.

---

1. See Foreword in *The Catholic Church and the Race Question* (Unesco).

Philosophy of an empiricist sort there is in Buddhism—as for instance the almost Humean analysis of the self and the rejection of the concept of the pure ego. But to consider Buddhism as a speculative metaphysics, which carries with it the connotation that it was a product of deductive reasoning based on self-evident axioms and premises is quite wrong. It is true that Buddhism gives a general account of the nature of existence and seeks to define man's place in it, but this account is claimed to be a product of vision and not of speculation.

Another reason why it is misleading to call Buddhism a philosophy is that it is not an abstract account of reality, for the acceptance of its philosophy (if we may call it so) implies a way of life which seeks to transform oneself as well as one's fellow beings—which constitutes the religion of Buddhism. It seeks not merely to interpret the world but to change it, so that the theory of Buddhism cannot be divorced from its practice. Its view of life implies necessarily a way of life.

OUTLINE OF THIS PAMPHLET

In the first chapter we propose briefly to outline the problems of race and racism and to indicate in what guises they arose in India prior to the rise of Buddhism. In the second chapter we shall discuss the Buddhist attitude to the problems of race, racial prejudice and allied problems. The third chapter will give a brief sketch of the historical attempt on the part of Buddhism to transcend the barriers of race and caste and bring people together, and the degree of success it attained by employing the weapons of gentle persuasion and example and never the power of the sword. The last chapter will contain our conclusions.

THE PROBLEMS OF RACE, RACISM AND CASTE

The problems of race and racism spring from attempts or assumptions on the part of people, consciously or unconsciously made, which result in regarding mankind as being divided on biological, or even sociological, grounds into a hierarchy of groups, among whom the allegedly 'superior' groups do no wrong in discriminating against the allegedly 'inferior' groups, thus hindering or preventing a harmonious relationship between human beings as a whole. These assumptions received a conscious formulation at the hands of the natural historians of the eighteenth and early nineteenth centuries, who classified men into different races which could be graded like species of animals into higher and lower. These racial myths, which were exploded by the later scientific biologists, nevertheless seem to have had a close connexion with the economic and imperial policy of European colonial powers, which often made them an excuse for exploiting overseas territories.

'Coloured' people were considered to be mentally underdeveloped and therefore incapable of looking after themselves in the modern industrial age. They were the 'white man's burden' and their welfare was a responsibility of the white man who had a right to govern them as he thought fit. The racial argument was not of course the only rationalization resorted to, for where there was some acknowledged affinity of 'race' between the conqueror and the conquered other 'reasons', such as the necessity of spreading Christianity or civilization, were adduced in support of the policy of economic and imperialist expansion. As Lord Acton says: 'The history of the organization and administration of the Punjab is a practical lesson upon the duties of the English Government in its Oriental possessions. We have to accomplish a change both in the state and in society to supersede the traditional government and the traditional civilization. Indian culture, though it was developed by the same Aryan race to which our civilization is indebted, has been arrested in its progress. Its law has been identified with its religion and therefore religion has tied down the people to the social usages and opinions which were current when the laws were first reduced to a code. The religion and manners of the Orientals mutually support one another; neither can be changed without the other. Hence the pioneer of civilization has to get rid of the religion of India to enable him to introduce a better culture and the pioneer of Christianity has to get rid of the Indian culture before he can establish his religion.' [1]

But the problems of race cannot be considered merely as a product of errant natural historians or of some of the German scholars who were convinced that the Nordic peoples were superior to the rest of mankind in intellectual and cultural endowment. Nor can we say that they arose with European colonial expansion. Racial prejudice is found everywhere in history where people identified race with the cultural group to which they belonged and regarded outsiders as aliens and barbarians who were not only considered to be uncultured but incapable of culture. Whenever such a group was led by economic and imperial ambitions to subjugate another group, which was different not only in cultural attainment but in physical appearance as well, racial prejudice seems to have reared its head and left its mark on future generations, even where the subjugation was complete and there was passive acquiescence on the part of the conquered. The phenomenon of caste in India, if only due to its uniqueness, is probably to be traced to a multiplicity of factors, some of which are peculiar to the Indian context, but much of caste prejudice probably had its origin in the racial prejudices of the race-conscious fair-skinned Aryans trying to suppress and administer the dark-skinned aborigines. In any case, the analogy between race prejudice and discrimination and the prejudice and discrimination within the hierarchy of castes is so close that the case against the former is applicable to the latter—and vice versa.

Although tensions and conflicts between members of different racial groups cannot be confined to any specific era in human history, it is significant that according to modern biologists there are no absolute racial groups warranting the concept of (different) species within mankind. Biologists are generally agreed not only that men are derived from a common stock but that they form one species. Of course, even if there were different species, there would not be any ethical grounds for

---

1. Lord Acton, *The Rambler*, May 1882, p. 534.

20

inter-racial prejudice and discrimination, but the biological unity of mankind certainly makes the case for the spiritual unity of mankind stronger.

If mankind is thus one species and all men are related, however distantly, through intermarriage among ancestors and the whole human race contains one pool of hereditary units or genes, a race within such a community becomes a relative concept. Genetically, races would have formed with the effects of time and environment, owing to biological isolation out of smaller communities between which there was little or no intermarriage, and thus in 'the anthropological sense the word race should be reserved for groups of mankind possessing well-developed and primarily heritable physical differences from other groups'.[1] These physical differences such as skin colour, hair form, shape of head, etc., would be the criteria which physical anthropologists adopt for the classification of races.

Yet what is more important is not whether there are or are not races in this modified biological sense of the term but whether people believe that there are, and it seems to be the case that the word 'race' is more often than not used in a loose sense to refer to a national group (Americans), a religious group (Jews), a linguistic group (Sinhalese), a cultural group (Europeans) or even a geographical group (Icelanders). This gives a cultural sense of race for the sociologist, and the root cause of much misunderstanding and illegitimate inferences seem to be the confusion of a cultural sense with the biological sense, resulting in the naive assumption that a different cultural group is also a different biological group.

RACISM

It may be worth while to indicate briefly the nature and forms of racial prejudice and discrimination, especially since we propose to bring out the analogies with caste prejudice and discrimination. The set of beliefs and practices which constitute racial prejudice and discrimination are now often referred to by the word 'racism'. As a set of beliefs it subscribes to the theory that mankind is composed of different genetically constituted races which have more or less retained their purity. Not only are the physical characteristics of people

---

1. *The Race Concept* (Unesco), p. 11.

born to these races determined by the genetic constitution of each, but even the mental qualities as well. No Negro, it would be held, can ever hope to be born without curly hair or a dark skin; and his mental capacity too would be on the whole below that of the Whites, and as this too is due to heredity it can no more be changed than his skin colour.

It would also be held that these different races would fall into a hierarchy as regards their superiority and inferiority. True representatives of the one race, the master race which is superior, would regard the other races as inferior in most respects. They would be considered inferior in their physique or physical type, and it would be held that while there would be more deformed and misshapen specimens among the 'inferior' races the aesthetically and physically perfect specimens of humanity would be found only within the master race. But much more obnoxious than the attitude to the physical appearance would be the denial of great capacity for intellectual and moral attainment or cultural development on the part of the 'inferior' races. Nor in specific abilities such as musical skill, linguistic ability, etc., would a high standard of achievement, equivalent to that of the 'superior race be attainable by members of the 'inferior' races. On the other hand, acquired traits due largely to social background and upbringing would be considered to be inborn. Closely associated with this doctrine that the mental characteristics and the human qualities of people are genetically determined is the ban on inter-racial marriage, on the supposed grounds that the biological crossing of the races results in degenerate children or hybridization.

The practical outcome of such beliefs, consciously or unconsciously held, is racial discrimination. It may take many forms:

1. The denial of the equality of political opportunity. Subject races are considered unfit to rule or manage their own affairs. At best, they are considered late developers in this art so that they have to be trained for long periods before they can be safely entrusted with this responsibility.
2. The denial of the equality of economic opportunity. The more responsible and better paid jobs cannot be given to members of a subject race, because of their alleged incapacity. Even where this is possible they should be paid less.
3. The denial of the equality of social opportunity. The subject races are sometimes denied the opportunity of

higher education and numerous social amenities enjoyed by the ruling 'superior' races.

4. The denial of freedom of worship. Free entry to places of worship, some of which nominally claim to preach the brotherhood of man, is denied to people with 'inferior' racial origins and sometimes where there is legal prohibition of this, social pressure prevents the law from being enforceable.

5. The denial of equality before the law. Subject races are dealt with differently for the same offence under the criminal or civil law. In extreme cases, as happened with the Jews under Nazism, there is denial of the right of property—or even the right to live.

All these disabilities which the races considered 'inferior' have to suffer are perpetrated by means of political, legal, educational, social and sometimes religious sanctions. All such beliefs, attitudes and practices are associated with the extreme forms of racism.

CASTE PREJUDICE AND RACE PREJUDICE

Before we proceed to draw analogies between caste and race prejudice it should be mentioned that caste was considered largely responsible for the stability of Indian society. As Hutton says: 'Geographical circumstances have imposed a certain unity on the inhabitants of the peninsula, whereas the diverse origins of the people have dictated variety. The view put forward in this volume is that it is caste which has made it possible for both requirements to be satisfied within a single social system, a system moreover which has proved historically to be very stable.'[1] It is also necessary to add that caste differences are not so easily noticed as differences in physical appearance and manner, which are taken as evidence for underlying racial differences, and again it is important to note that the so-called 'inferor' castes did not always resent or take up arms against the discrimination against them. They not only humbly acquiesced for the most part in their lot but took care by observing their own caste rules to maintain and perpetuate a system which placed their members at such a disadvantage in the context of society as a whole. But with the spread of secular education these

1. J. H. Hutton, *Caste in India* (Oxford, Univ. Press, 1951), p. 1.

values are fast changing and whatever the historical role the institution of caste may have played in the past the time has come to recognize caste prejudices and discrimination for what they are, so as to prevent caste barriers from hindering harmonious relations between fellow men.

Although differences of physical type are not clearly observable as between different castes, the fact that castes were endogamous units, has, quite apart from other historical reasons, probably resulted in the several caste groups maintaining different proportions of the same kinds of genes—a fact which can be ascertained by studying the relative distribution of blood types within these groups; since the distribution of genes is said to determine certain properties of the blood. As L. C. Dunn says in his booklet on *Race and Biology*, 'blood typing immediately reveals the genetic constitution of the person tested, so that the distribution of these genes in a population is known from the blood group distribution'.[1] The results of such blood tests on two caste groups are worth quoting here: 'These differences in proportions are racial differences, that is, they indicate partial separation of the population in which the different proportions are maintained. The differences may be just as great between populations living in the same city at between populations living half a world away from each other. In Table V [of that booklet] are shown the blood group varieties in the two caste communities in Bombay, as determined by two Indian investigators:

	O	A	B	AB
Indians (Bombay G.K.P.)[1]	34.5	28.5	28.5	8.5
Indians (Bombay K.B.)[2]	51.0	24	20	5.0

1. Members of the caste community Chandraseniya Kayasth Prabhu.
2. Members of the caste community Koknasth Brahman.

The blood types of these two groups are quite different, and differences like this were also found in six other gene-determined characters. They are in fact at least as different in these traits as American Whites and American Negroes, who are separated by the low frequency of intermarriages. These Indian communities are separated by customs which

---

1. *Race and Biology* (Unesco), p. 31.

24

allow marriages to be contracted only between members of certain specified sections within the caste.

'These conditions permit the maintenance of gene differences between the groups. No one hesitates to call such differences 'racial' as between Whites and Negroes, everyone being aware that the ancestors of the Negroes came from Africa a few hundred years ago, where they had been practically isolated from European plantations. But there would be a good deal of hesitation in referring to the two Indian caste communities as belonging to different races.'[1]

Whether this genetic difference between these two caste groups is due to the operation of caste endogamy in historical times, or has an earlier racial origin which was more or less maintained, is not a point on which we wish to be dogmatic; but it is interesting to note that Risley,[2] who argued for the racial origin of caste, observed after comparing the nasal indices of some of the castes of Hindustan that the order of gradation established by means of the nasal index is substantially the same as that of social precedence. The point we wish to make is that, by prohibiting intermarriage between castes, caste groups operate genetically like racial groups and it is possible that if such isolation is perpetuated caste groups may in time exhibit visibly different racial types.

There is a close analogy between prejudice and discrimination as operative in caste on the one hand and race relations on the other. As we shall attempt to show in the next chapter how Early Buddhism fought such prejudice and discrimination, we shall draw our illustrations mostly from the example of ancient India. Just as racism divides mankind into a hierarchy of genetically different and mutually exclusive groups and forbids intermarriage on the ground that it is biologically undesirable, caste too divides mankind into a hierarchy of groups genetically determined and fixed, and strongly condemns intermarriage on pain of severe penalties, on the ground that it is biologically or socially undesirable. Just as there are 'superior' and 'inferior' races within the hierarchy of racial groups, there are here the 'superior' and 'inferior' caste groups.

As in the case of the 'superior' race, the 'superior' caste would regard the 'lower' castes as inferior in all respects. The members of the 'lower' castes were considered to be

---

1. ibid., pp. 31, 32.
2. *Anthropometric Data from Bengal* (1891).

physically ugly, loathsome and deformed; while the 'superi-
or' castes were handsome and charming. The men of 'low'
castes like the 'Chandalas, Nesadas, basket-weavers, chariot-
makers or Pukkusas' are described as 'black, ill-featured,
hunch-backed, a prey to many diseases, purblind or with
a crooked hand, lame or paralysed', while the 'higher' castes,
'the Ksatriyas (rulers), Brahmins (priests) and householders',
are described as 'handsome, fair-looking and charming'.[1]
But much more reprehensible is the fact that the Sudras
(lowest castes, outcasts) were, in the opinion of the 'high
castes', by birth and nature intellectually and morally defi-
cient as well. As Ghurye observes: 'Manu declares roundly
that a Sudra cannot commit an offence causing loss of his
caste, so degraded was he. Where some kinds of spirituous
liquors are forbidden to the members of the twice-born castes,
the Sudra is left to himself. Evidently the Sudra was regarded
beyond the pale of moral influence. The Brahmin did not
even condescend to expect of him an adherence to his high
moral precepts.'[2] The Sathapatha Brahmana goes so far
as to say that a Sudra (outcast) is untruth itself.[3] His
acquired traits, like the services he rendered and which were
almost invariably of a menial character, were considered to
be inborn. The Sudra is always born to be the servant of
another.[4] The analogy with the attitude of the 'superior'
race to the 'inferior' is almost complete.

The practical outcome of such beliefs and attitudes was,
as in the case of racism, discrimination against and the
exploitation of the 'lower' castes. If we may follow the
items we listed under racism we can speak of:

1. The denial of equality of political opportunity. It was
   unthinkable, in the opinion of the 'higher' castes, that
   the members of the 'lower' castes should be considered
   fit to govern and administer the country (the duty of the
   Ksatriyas) or to render the rulers advice (the duty of the
   Brahmins). Even if a Sudra mentions the name and class
   of the twice-born arrogantly, an iron nail ten fingers long
   shall be thrust red hot into his mouth.[5] If he proudly

---

1. Though the quotation is from a Buddhist text which argues that both
   are equally capable of moral or immoral behaviour, it reflects the prevailing
   attitude. B. C. Law, *Human Types* (Pali Text Society), pp. 70, 71.
2. *Caste and Race in India* (London, 1932), p. 84.
3. Eggeling's Translation, Pt. V, p. 446.
4. Aitareya Brahmana VII. 29.
5. 'The Laws of Manu' (trans. Buhler), *Sacred Books of the East*, Vol. XXV,
   VIII. 271.

26

teaches Brahmins (priests) their duty the king shall cause hot oil to be poured into his mouth and into his ears.[1] But no reciprocal punishments are prescribed for Brahmins who follow mean occupations.

2. The denial of equality of economic opportunity. In ancient India, especially in those regions where Brahminism most strongly prevailed, the Sudra was not only considered the servant of another but also regarded as one who could be expelled at will and slain at will, thus showing that he had no rights to property or even life against the king. The Laws of Manu say 'A Sudra, whether bought or unbought, may be compelled to do servile work; for he was created by the Self-Existent to be the slave of a Brahmin'.[2] Servitude was regarded as an innate quality of the Sudra who is incapable of altering his genetic constitution, which makes him so. 'A Sudra though emancipated by his master is not released from servitude; since that is innate in him, who can set him free from it?'[3]

3. The denial of equality of social opportunity. A man born to be a slave and a servant of another cannot expect to receive any social opportunities for self-advancement and amelioration. Education was denied him. A Brahmin 'who instructs Sudra pupils' was penalized.[4] Brahmins should not even recite the texts in the presence of Sudras.[5] There is no objection to Sudras imitating the practice of virtuous men, but they should do so 'without reciting sacred texts'.[6] The rules of untouchability prevented the Sudra from being at ease in his social environment; free access to wells and sometimes even the use of roads was denied to him.

4. The denial of religious freedom. A Brahmin who 'explains the sacred law [to a Sudra] or dictates to him a penance will sink together with that man into the hell called Asamvrta'.[7] Not only was the Sudra (outcast) denied access to religious instruction, he had no right, unlike the 'superior' castes (i.e., Brahmins, Ksatriyas and Vaisyas), to be initiated[8] or to have religious ceremonies performed

---

1. ibid., VIII. 272.
2. ibid., VIII. 413.
3. ibid., VIII. 414.
4. ibid., III. 156.
5. ibid., IV. 99.
6. ibid., X. 128.
7. ibid., IV. 81.
8. ibid., X. 4.

for him.[1] Denied access to sacred knowledge and the right to perform religious ceremonies for himself, it was, according to some of the Early Brahmanical accounts, unimaginable that a Sudra should attain salvation. The refusal of temple entry to Sudras is among the consequences of a restrictive policy which denied religious participation to the Sudras.

5. The denial of equality before the law. Both in the criminal and civil procedures there was unequal treatment meted out to the Sudra, who had to undergo greater disabilities than his fellow men of the 'higher' castes. A Sudra committing homicide or theft suffered confiscation of his property and capital punishment,[2] but a Brahmin was only blinded for such crimes.[3] Even in matters outside the criminal law, we find, for instance, that the rate of interest charged was disproportionately high for a Sudra, although he was the poorest in the social scale. Vasistha states that 'two, three, four, five in the hundred is declared in the Smrti to be the monthly interest according to caste'.[4]

If we compare the beliefs, attitudes and modes of discrimination and exploitation embodied in racism with the corresponding beliefs, attitudes and practices of caste prejudice and discrimination, it will thus be seen that the analogy between the two is a particularly close one. The only difference, apart from the historical role of caste as a stabilizing agency for society, is that the prejudice and discrimination on the basis of caste has been legalized and given religious sanction and—presumably—accepted by all parties for this and other historical reasons.

RACIAL ORIGIN OF CASTE PREJUDICE?

In view of the close analogy between race and caste prejudice and their effects, it is of little consequence for our purposes here whether caste prejudices originated in whole or part in racial prejudices or not. But it is interesting to note that the majority of scholars who have offered theories or suggestions about the origins of caste have admitted the important

---

1. ibid., III. 183.
2. *Apastamba Dharmasutra*, ii. 16, 27.
3. ibid., 17.
4. Quoted from R. K. Mookerji, *Hindu Civilisation* (1936), p. 138.

contribution made by the racial contact between the Aryan invader and the non-Aryan aborigine and the prejudices resulting from it—even though they were not always willing to trace caste prejudices and practices in their entirety to the initial racial prejudices of the Aryan invader in his attempt to suppress and subjugate a different race of people.[1]

Risley[2] was one of the first to trace caste to racial origins and explain the genesis of caste in terms of the prejudices of racial contact and hypergamy. Hutton has the following interesting comments to make on this hypothesis which, incidentally, show a parallel with the history of the treatment of Negroes in the southern states of the U.S.A.: 'In order to base caste on hypergamy Risley finds it necessary to pre-suppose a hypothetical point at which the result of inter-marriage between fair invaders and dark aborigines provides enough women for the society in question to close its ranks and become a caste, although there still exist outside it more women of the same community from which it has been drawing its wives and with which it has been in more or less intimate relation. The position of Negroes in the southern states of the U.S.A. has been cited as offering a parallel case and the view is supported by Westermarck; it finds a certain measure of confirmation perhaps, in the laws passed in the Union of South Africa against the intermarriage of white and coloured races; but it fails to offer any satisfactory explanation of the taboo on commensality'.[3] As regards this taboo and the phenomenon of untouchability Hutton sees an analogy where he grants that 'separate railway carri-ages, separate restaurants and even separate townships are provided for Negroes'[4] and even goes on to illustrate in a footnote[4] that the concept of pollution is not totally foreign to the American context. Hutton's theory is that 'the prim-itive conceptions of taboo, mana and soul stuff'[5] are neces-sary to account for the concepts of caste contamination and pollution and that they cannot be accounted for in terms of racial prejudice or of racial prejudice alone. But it must be borne in mind that just as much as in the American context 'no pollution takes place as a result of employing Negro

---

1. For a discussion and summary of these views see Hutton, op. cit., Chap. XI.
2. Risley, *The Peoples of India*.
3. op. cit., pp. 172-3.
4. ibid.
5. op. cit., p. 181.

servants' in ancient India as well no pollution took place as a result of Brahmins employing Sudra servants.

The strength of the racial hypothesis lies in the fact that it can explain so many factors of caste prejudice. It has some literary evidence to back it. It also finds confirmation in the anthropometric analyses of the caste groups of North India.[1] The Rigveda sometimes gives vivid accounts of what the Aryan felt among the aborigines among whom he had to settle down. One hymn says: 'We are surrounded on all sides by Dasyu tribes. They do not perform sacrifices; they do not believe in anything. They are not men! O destroyer of foes! Kill them. Destroy the Dasa race'.[2] We find here the usual pre-conditions of racial prejudice. The migrant invaders have encountered a tribe of people who are considered to be racially and culturally different. The physical differences are striking. The aborigines are dark-skinned and noseless (*anāsa*). They have a different language and a different religion, in short a different culture; their intentions do not appear to be too peaceful even after the subjugation and they are described as 'revilers of Vedic gods (*deva-pīyu*)'. They were an 'out-group' from the point of view of religion, as is evident from the usual epithets used to refer to them. They were devoid of Vedic rituals (*akar-man*), not worshipping Vedic gods (*adevayu*), non-sacrificing (*ayajvan*), phallus-worshippers (*siṣṇa-devāh*), lawless (*avrata*), lacking devotion (*abrahman*), followers of strange ordinances (*anya-vrata*), and as such were not men and deserve to be destroyed. In fact, if we substitute 'Aryan' for 'European' and 'Vedic religion' for 'Christianity', the following words of Little,[3] would aptly describe the situation: 'The way of life of these migrants was strongly opposed to the cultural systems which they encountered; therefore the native inhabitants had to be suppressed whenever they obstructed or threatened to obstruct the European (Aryan) purpose. This suppression was frequently carried out in the early days with relative rapidity and with but few scruples, on the ground that the native people constituted an 'out-group' from the point of view of Christianity (Vedic religion).'

If there is a basic similarity between the nature of caste prejudice and discrimination and of racial prejudice and

---

1. Risley, *Anthropometric Data from Bengal* (1891).
2. Rigveda, X. 22. 8.
3. *Race and Society* (Unesco), p. 50.

discrimination, and if it is also likely that it was these racial prejudices which became congealed in the caste prejudices of a later day—to which the word for caste or *varna* which means 'skin colour' still appears to bear witness—then in combating these latter prejudices we are dealing with the problem of racism in another form, and objections against either caste or racism would be *ipso facto* objections against the other.

THE BUDDHIST CONCEPTION OF MAN AND THE ATTITUDE TO RACISM AND CASTE

MAN'S PLACE IN THE UNIVERSE

The texts of both the Theravāda (i.e., the southern) as well as of the Mahāyāna (i.e., the northern) schools of Buddhism often speak of man in the context of a larger concourse of sentient beings who are considered as populating a vast universe. Although speculations about the origin and extent of the universe are discouraged, the vastness of space and the immensity of time are never lost sight of. It is said that, even if one moves with the swiftness of an arrow in any direction and travel for a whole lifetime, one can never hope to reach the limits of space.[1] In this vastness of cosmic space are located an innumerable number of worlds. 'As far as these suns and moons revolve, shedding their light in space, so far extends the thousandfold world-system. In it are a thousand suns, a thousand moons, thousands of earths and thousands of heavenly worlds. This is said to be the thousandfold minor world-system. A thousand times such a thousandfold minor world-system is the twice-a-thousand middling world-system. A thousand times such a twice-a-thousand middling world-system is the thrice-a-thousand major world-system.'[2] These galactic systems (if we may use a modern term which seems to approximate very closely to this conception of the world systems) are however never static or lasting; they are in the process of being evolved (*samvaṭṭamāna*), or of being dissolved (*vivaṭṭamāna*). These processes take immensely long periods of time measured in aeons (*kappa*).[3] until eventually cosmic catastrophes put an end to them.[4] But time, we are told, is not the same everywhere, for fifty earth years are equivalent to one day and night in one of the heavenly worlds, while in another a day

---

1. A. IV. 428.
2. A. I. 227, 228; IV. 59, 60.
3. S. II. 181.
4. A. IV. 100-3.

and night is equivalent to no less than 1,600 earth years.[1]

Several attempts are made to classify this vast array of beings. One such classification speaks of human beings, as well as some of the higher and lower beings, as falling into the class of beings who are different and distinguishable from each other in mind and body. There are other classes where the beings are different in body but one in mind. Yet others are alike in body but different in mind, while there are some who are alike both in body and in mind. A further set of four classes of beings are mentioned who are formless. All these are described as the several stations which the human consciousness can attain (*vinnanatthiti*),[2] and find renewed existence after death. Another such classification puts beings into the several classes of the 'no-footed, the two-footed, the four-footed, the many-footed, those having or lacking material form, the conscious, the unconscious and the super-conscious[3]. The human worlds are always represented as standing midway in the hierarchy of worlds. Life in these human worlds is a mixture of the pleasant and the unpleasant, the good and the evil, while the pleasant and good traits are intensified in the higher worlds and the unpleasant and evil in the lower.

If we contemplate the vastness of cosmic space and the seemingly endless number of worlds of which the human worlds form a very small part, the problems of race would appear in a different light and seem very trifling indeed. One is reminded of a comparison the Buddha made when he rebuked a section of his monks who felt superior to the rest in that they had more fame and gain than the others. He likens them to worms who, born in dung, bred in dung, and living on dung, feel superior to other worms who are not so privileged in this respect. Whatever the picture we may get from a cosmic perspective of humanity crawling over the surface of the earth and trying to eke out an existence on it, humility is one of the lessons we have to learn from it. 'Kingship on earth is a beggarly existence, in comparison with the joys of the heavenly worlds.'[4] The span of life of mortal men is insignificantly small in comparison with cosmic time and may be compared in its duration to a line drawn on the earth.[5]

---

1. A. IV. 429.
2. A. IV. 39, 40.
3. A. III. 35.
4. A. IV. 254.
5. A. IV. 138.

But although human life appears insignificant from a cosmic standpoint, yet it is constantly pointed out in the Buddhist texts as being of tremendous worth, as man has within him the capacity of gaining the highest knowledge or of attaining a moral pre-eminence which can make him worthy of becoming a 'ruler of a world system'. This is not possible for those in lower-than-human states of existence whose actions are instinctive and too preoccupied with securing elementary needs; nor is it possible for those in the higher worlds who are too distracted by the joys of the present for serious contemplation to be possible. This is why a human birth is so valuable although in the cosmic scheme of things it is all too rare. In the course of our samsaric [1] evolution we have been born, as it is said, hundreds of times as animals, [2] and it is rarely that we emerge into a human existence; 'birth as a human being is a rare event' (*dullabham manussattam*). It is therefore the duty of humans to make the most of the precious human life that they have acquired. Man has within him the potentiality of discovering the deepest truths about the cosmos for himself. A person who has realized such potentialities is the Buddha, who is not only the best among humans but the highest among all sentient beings. When the Buddha was asked whether he was man or god, he answered that he was neither since he was the Buddha. [3] The intellectual, moral and spiritual heights that man can attain are so great that those who have attained them are as different from ordinary men as men are from animals. Yet such men are not mere freaks nor have they been specially favoured by any divine agency. They have attained such heights by dint of effort directed towards developing their intellectual, moral and spiritual nature extending over many lives. And what has been achieved by one or a few is within the capacity of all to achieve. As the Mahāyāna texts put it, it is not only men but all sentient beings down to the very lowest who are potential Buddhas, in that a Buddha nature (*Buddha-bhāva*) is present within them. If only for this reason, no one has a right to despise a fellow creature, since all are subject to the same laws of existence and have ultimately the same nature and the same potentialities

---

1. *Samsara* is a technical term denoting the round of continued existence.
2. S. II. 188.
3. A. II. 38.

34

though they are in varying stages of growth or development
and their rates of growth may differ from time to time.

At the human level the lessons that man can learn by
realizing his position in the universe are not only that he needs
to be humble but also that he need not despair, since he has
the power to understand the world and overcome it and
cease to be a mere mechanism within it. Both these lessons,
the realization of our common plight as well as the potentialities within each of us, teach us but one moral—namely
that it is everyone's duty to help his fellow beings and that
no one has any right or valid grounds to despise another.

THE BIOLOGICAL UNITY OF MANKING AND THE CASE
AGAINST RACISM

A special emphasis is placed in Buddhism on the worth and
dignity of human existence in view of the opportunities and
potentialities that man possesses for self-development. The
unity of mankind is emphasized, and a distinction drawn
between human beings and the animal and plant kingdoms.

It is argued on biological grounds that—unlike in the case
of the plant and animal kingdoms, where differences of species
are noticeable—mankind is one species. This view accords
remarkably with the findings of modern biological science.
Not only is it in disagreement with the scientific pretensions
of the biologists of the eighteenth and early nineteenth
centuries, who tried to classify men into different races
which could be graded like species of animals into the higher
and lower, but it cuts the ground beneath the very foundations
of any racist doctrine which would divide human beings into
more or less isolated groups, and argue that their varying
human characteristics are in their entirety genetically determined. The following passage occurs in a polemic against
the pretensions of the Brahmanic caste theory and incidentally shows by implication how the Brahmins were claiming
superiority for themselves on genetical grounds:

'We have a controversy regarding [the distinctions of]
birth, O Gotama! Bharadvaja says, one is a Brahmin by
birth, and I say by deeds; know this, O thou clearly-seeing!

'We are both unable to convince each other, [therefore]
we have come to ask thee [who art] celebrated as perfectly
enlightened.'

'I will explain to you—O Vasettha', so said Bhagavat,

'in due order the exact distinction of living beings according to species, for their species are manifold.

'Know ye the grass and the trees, although they do not exhibit [it], the marks that constitute species are for them, and [their] species are manifold.

'Then know ye the worms, and the moths, and the different sorts of ants, the marks that constitute species are for them, and [their] species are manifold.

'Know ye also the four-footed [animals], small and great, the marks that constitute species are for them, and [their] species are manifold.

'Know ye also the serpents, the long-backed snakes, the marks that constitute species are for them, and [their] species are manifold.

'Then know ye also the fish which range in the water, the marks that constitute species are for them, and [their] species are manifold.

'Then know ye also the birds that are borne along on wings and move through the air, the marks that constitute species are for them, and [their] species are manifold.

'As in these species the marks that constitute species are abundant, so in men the marks that constitute species are not abundant.

'Not as regards their hair, head, ears, eyes, mouth, nose, lips, or brows,

'Nor as regards their neck, shoulders, belly, back, hip, breast, female organ, sexual intercourse,

'Nor as regards their hands, feet, palms, nails, calves, thighs, colour or voice are there marks that constitute species as in other species.

'Difference there is in beings endowed with bodies, but amongst men this is not the case, the difference amongst men is nominal [only].

'For whoever amongst men lives by cow-keeping—know this, O Vasettha—he is a husbandman, not a Brahmin.

'And whoever amongst men lives by archery—know this, O Vasettha—he is a soldier, not a Brahmin.

'And I do not call one a Brahmin on account of his birth or of his origin from a [particular] mother. . . .'[1]

What is apparent from the above is that, according to the Buddha, there are no distinguishing characteristics of genus and species among men, unlike in the case of grasses,

___

1. 'Sutta Nipata' (trans. Fausböll), *Sacred Books of the East*, Vol. X, pp. 111-13.

trees, worms, moths, fishes, beasts, birds, etc. As Chalmers says: 'Herein, Gotama was in accord with the conclusion of modern biologists that "the *Anthropidae* are represented by the single genus and species, Man"—a conclusion which was the more remarkable inasmuch as the accident of colour did not mislead Gotama.'[1] The Buddha goes on to show that the apparent divisions between men are not due to basic biological factors but are 'conventional classifications' (*samaññā*). The distinctions made in respect of the differences in skin colour (*vaṇṇa*), hair form (*kesa*), the shape of the head (*sīsa*) or the shape of the nose (*nāsa*), etc., are not absolute categories. One is almost reminded of the statement of the scientists that 'the concept of race is unanimously regarded by anthropologists as a *classificatory device* ....'[2]

It would thus appear that Buddhism is in accord with the findings of the modern biologists who exploded the doctrines of racism and would urge the biological unity of mankind in support of the concept of a common humanity. So when Buddhism asks us to treat all men, irrespective of race or caste, as our fathers, mothers, brothers and sisters or as one family, there seems to be a deeper truth in this statement than that of a mere ethical recommendation.

While the above passage brings out the Buddhist attitude to the problem of race, it is not possible to say that Early Buddhism was confronted with a racial problem as such. The problem was no doubt there in Rigvedic society, where the race-conscious Aryan who spoke derisively of the dark-skinned and noseless aborigines treated them as an inferior race. But by the time of the rise of Buddhism this race-consciousness had given place to a caste-consciousness and it was the Brahmin in particular and the 'higher' castes in general, who were probably derived largely from Aryan stock, who claimed superiority by virtue of their light skin colour. It was claimed by the Brahmins to be one of the hereditary characteristics of a Brahmin that he was 'handsome (*abhi-rūpo*), fair (*dassanīyo*), endowed with an excellent complexion (*paramāya vaṇṇa-pokkharatāya samannāgato*), and of the fairest colour (*brahma-vannī*)'[3] by virtue of which he claimed superiority over those of a dark complexion.

The terms 'Aryan' (*ariya*) and 'non-Aryan' (*anariya*) are

---

1. *Journal of the Royal Asiatic Society*, 1894, p. 346.
2. *The Race Concept* (Unesco), p. 33.
3. D. I. 119.

frequently found in the Buddhist texts, but never in a racial
sense. The racial sense of superiority associated with the
word 'Aryan' is completely eclipsed by the moral and spiritual
sense of superiority, which the word in a Buddhist context
connotes, devoid of any associations of race or birth. Thus
Angulimala, a brutal brigand and a person of a 'low' caste
who struck terror in the territory of the King of Kosala by
his wanton acts of cruelty, is described after being converted
by the Buddha as 'ariyāya jātiya jāto,' which means 'reborn
with a spiritual birth', though if the words are taken literally
the phrase would mean 'born in the Aryan race'. The use
of the word 'Aryan' in the sense of 'noble' and 'spiritual'
and 'non-Aryan' in the sense of 'ignoble' and 'immoral' is
an eloquent testimony of how Buddhism ignored racial claims
and distinctions. Thus 'Aryan quest' (*ariyā pariyesanā*)
means 'spiritual quest', which is defined as 'the quest of one
who being subject to birth, decay and death realizes the
evil consequences thereof and seeks the immortal and secure
haven of Nirvana'.[1] The 'Aryan haven' (*ariyā uccāsayana-
mahāsayanam*) means the 'spiritual haven', which is 'the
state of being free from lust, hatred and delusion'.[2]

There is, however, a philosophical theory of 'racism' held
by some of the religious teachers in the Buddha's time which
is mentioned and criticised in the Buddhist texts. It is
associated with two teachers both of whom denied free will
to man. One was Purana Kassapa, who denied man's capacity for moral action in virtue of the fact that he had no
free will. The other was Makkhali Gosala, who denied both
free will and causation and argued that beings were miraculously saved (*ahetu appaccayā sattā visujjhanti*) or doomed.
They argued that human beings belonged to one or another
of six species (*abhijāti*)[3] or specific types; in virtue of which
they had certain genetic constitutions, physical traits and
habits and psychological natures which they were incapable
of altering by their own will or effort. The six types were
designated by six colours. They were the black species
(*kanhābhijāti*), the blue species, the red species, the yellow
species, the white species and the pure white species. Whether
these colours denoted differences in their physical complexions

---

1. M. I. 162-3.
2. A. I. 182.
3. A. III. 383-4.

38

is not clear, [1] but that they were genetically different physical and psychological types is what is implied by the classification. To the black species belonged the butchers, fowlers, hunters, fishermen, dacoits, and executioners and all those who adopt a cruel mode of living. They were, incidentally, among the lowest castes and their complexion was on the whole the darkest. The other five specific types differed in virtue of their degree of wickedness or saintliness, which was not in their power to alter. The pure white species were reckoned to be the perfect saints, though their saintliness was considered to be natural to them as much as their physical constitutions, and was in no way achieved by any effort of will on their part. In the opinion of these typologists, human beings who suffered pain in this life were so born to suffer as a result of their inheriting certain physical constitutions and psychological natures. [2]

Arguing from the reality of free will and the capacity that man has within himself of becoming either moral or immoral or even happy or unhappy by transforming himself or degenerating morally as the case may be, the Buddha denies that there are such fixed human types genetically determined. There are no men who are intrinsically good or evil by nature and must necessarily remain so, for the evil can turn into good and the good degenerate into evil. The six types of human beings that the Buddha would recognize do not have fixed natures genetically determined but are the six classes of beings, namely the evil who remain evil, the evil who become good, the evil who transcend good and evil (and enter Nirvana), the good who become evil, the good who remain good and the good who transcend both good and evil (and enter Nirvana)—all of them no doubt by the exercise of their free will. The emphasis is not on what a man is born with but what he does with himself since man, irrespective of his physical constitution and psychological nature at birth, can—given the opportunity and effort—change for better or worse. The racist tenor of the former theory is thus denounced in the Buddha's classification, where the merits of people are to be judged not in terms of what they are born with but what they do with themselves.

---

1. cf. Mahabharata. Santiparvan, where it is said that 'the colour of the Brahmin was white, that of the Ksatriyas red, that of the Vaisyas yellow and that of the Sudras black'. The commentator, however, explains these colours as psychological characteristics in terms of Samkhya philosophy.
2. M. II. 222.

Although it should be clear from the above that Buddhism
upholds the biological unity of mankind and denies any
genetical basis for discrimination between different 'racial'
groups, it may be noted that the statements about race quoted
above were not made in an encounter with any racial problem
as such, for the racial conflict between the Aryan and non-
Aryan had been reduced in the time of the Buddha mainly
to a caste conflict between the Brahmins or the 'higher'
castes versus the 'lower'. It is in such a context that the
problem is generalized and discussed in the background of
the biological doctrines which caste theory appeared to
espouse or take for granted.

In the last chapter we referred to the possible racial origin
of much of caste prejudice, and showed the strong similarity
between the prejudice and discrimination in matters of caste
as in race. The case against caste discrimination and prejudice as presented in Buddhism applies as much against
caste as against racial prejudice and discrimination.

The course that Buddhism adopted in combating caste
prejudice and discrimination was to ignore it in practice and
denounce its theory by means of rational persuasion. We
shall take up the former aspect of the question in the next
chapter and confine ourselves here to the scientific, ethical
and religious arguments adduced against the theory of caste
as advanced by the Brahmins. The scientific arguments may
conveniently be classified as the biological and the sociological.

The Biological Arguments

The thesis that we do not find differences of species among
human beings as we do among plants and animals and that
mankind is one species forms the crux of the biological
argument. Found in the earliest texts (as quoted above),
this argument is expanded in subsequent polemics against
caste written by Buddhists. Thus Asvaghosa in his *Vajrasūci*
(*circa* first century A.D.) says:

'All that I have said about Brahmins you must know is
equally applicable to Kshatriyas; and that the doctrine of
the four castes is altogether false. All men are of one caste.

'Wonderful! You affirm that all men proceeded from one,

i.e. Brahma; how then can there be a fourfold insuperable diversity among them? If I have four sons by one wife, the four sons having one father and mother must be all essentially alike. Know too that distinctions of race among beings are broadly marked by differences of conformations and organization. Thus, the foot of the elephant is very different from that of the horse; that of the tiger unlike that of the deer: and so of the rest, and by that single diagnosis we learn that those animals belong to very different races. But I never heard that the foot of a Kshatriya was different from that of a Brahmin or that of a Sudra. All men are formed alike, and are clearly of one race. Further, the generative organs, the colour, the figure, the ordure, the urine, the odour and the utterance of the ox, the buffalo, the horse, the elephant, the ass, the monkey, the goat, the sheep, etc., furnish further diagnostics whereby to separate these various races of animals: but in all those respects the Brahmin resembles the Kshatriya, and is therefore of the same race or species with him. I have instanced among quadrupeds the diversities which separate diverse genera. I now proceed to give some more instances from among birds. Thus, the goose, the dove, the parrot, the peacock, etc., are known to be different by their diversities of figure, and colour, and plumage and beak; but the Brahmin, Kshatriya, Vaishya and Sudra are alike without and within. How then can we say they are essentially distinct? Again, among trees, the Vata and Bakula, and Palasha and Ashoka, the Tamala and Nagakeshara, and Shirisha and Champaka and others, are clearly contradistinguished by their stems, and leaves, and flowers, and fruits and barks, and timber, and seeds, and juices and odours; but Brahmins, and Kshatriyas and the rest, are alike in flesh, and skin, and blood, and bones, and figure, and excrements, and mode of birth. It is surely then clear that they are of one species or race. Again, tell me, is a Brahmin's sense of pleasure and pain different from that of a Kshatriya? Does not the one sustain life in the same way, and find death from the same causes as the other? Do they differ in intellectual faculties, in their actions or the objects of those actions; in the manner of their birth or in their subjection to fear and hope? Not a whit. It is therefore clear that they are essentially the same. In the Udumbara and Panasa trees the fruit is produced from the branches, the stem, the joints and the roots. Is one fruit therefore different from another, so that we may call that produced

from the top of the stem the Brahmin fruit, and that from
the roots the Sudra fruit? Surely not. Nor can men be of
four distinct races because they sprang from four different
parts of one body.'[1]

The differences in skin colour (*vaṇṇa*), hair (*kesa*), shape
of nose (*nāsa*), or head (*sīsa*) were indeed small in comparison
with the differences among the various species of plants and
animals. Caste names were merely conventional designations
signifying occupational differences and, since men were free
to change their occupations, these differences had no hereditary or genetical basis. As Asvaghosa says, 'The distinctions between Brahmins, Kshatriyas, Vaishyas and Sudras
are founded merely on the observance of diverse rites and
the practice of different professions.'[2] One who engages in
trade comes to be known as a merchant, one who indulges
in military pursuits is known as a soldier, and one who admin-
isters the country a king. It was not by birth that one
becomes merchant, soldier or king but by the actions that
one performs or the job one does.

Caste theory tried early to lay down that there were specific
hereditary occupations (*karma*) suitable for people born into
the different castes, and since they had a special aptitude
(*guṇa*) for these types of occupations it was the specific duty
(*svadharma*) or obligation of those born in their respective
castes to perform their respective tasks and no others. A
son of Sudra (outcast) parents must always do a menial job
for which he has been created with a special aptitude, and
the son of Ksatriya parents an administrative job. Even
the Bhagavadgita says: 'The fourfold order was created by
Me [i.e. God] according to the divisions of quality and work',[3]
meaning thereby that God created the four castes with certain aptitudes (*guṇa*) and functions (*karma*) and it was their
duty to perform their respective functions and not swerve
from this path of duty.

The analogy with racist theory is that the 'superior' races
are born to rule, with a special aptitude for this task, while
the 'inferior' races are born to serve their masters who rule
them. It was such a theory that Buddhism denounced, on
the grounds that it had no basis in fact since people are not
born in their respective castes with such aptitudes gene-

---

1. Quoted from H. H. Wilson, *Indian Caste* (London, 1877), pp. 302-3.
2. ibid., pp. 303-4.
3. *The Bhagavadgita* (London, 1948), ed. Radhakrishnan, p. 160.

tically determined and are under no obligation to do the work assigned to their castes and no other. The job one does and that one is free to choose should give one's 'caste' name (*kammana khattiyo, vasalo... hoti*), but it is merely a conventional designation denoting one's occupation and is of no genetical significance, since one does not follow a vocation or have an aptitude for it merely because one was born of parents who followed the same. [1]

Man is biologically one species. There are no separate castes (or races) radically different from each other and created from the beginning. The concept of pure castes (analogous to that of pure races) is dismissed on the grounds that most of us cannot in the least be sure whether caste purity, or intermarriage strictly within the caste alone, was observed by our parents and grandparents even up to seven generations. [2] Devala the Dark, who is quoted as one of the Brahmin seers opposed to the caste theory formulated by some of the Rigvedic Brahmins, questions the latter in the course of a discussion about caste as to whether they remember whether their parents and grandparents were of the same caste even up to seven generations; to which it is replied that they do not. It is then concluded that in such circumstances 'We do not know who we are' (*na mayam jānāma keci mayam homa*) [3] and therefore we have no right to maintain the reality or purity of castes. We also find the Buddha arguing with Brahmins who claimed caste purity, showing them that some of their ancestors did not marry within the caste [4] and that the claim to purity was therefore a myth and not a fact.

It also follows from the biological unity of mankind that intermarriage between castes or races is both possible and not necessarily undesirable. This was again a point on which the caste theorists, like the racists, held strong views— severely condemning intermarriage between castes on the ground that this would have disastrous consequences. The Buddha on the other hand not only argued against claims to caste purity in view of the fact that intermarriage between castes was both a possibility and a historical fact, but even seems to have held that it was not necessarily undesirable. The

---

1. Sn. 650.
2. D. I. 92-9.
3. M. II. 156.
4. Ambattha Sutta Digha Nikaya.

products of such caste mixture would resemble both parents and in such situations we cannot say from observing the physical or genetical constitutions to which caste the child belongs.

The Ambattha Sutta[1] (i.e., the Discourse on Ambattha) exposes the myth of the purity of caste of which the Brahmins were so conscious. Ambattha was a Brahmin youth who was so conscious of his high Brahmin lineage that he did not observe the usual courtesies in talking to the Buddha, whom he despised on the score that he was not a Brahmin. In the course of the conversation with him, which turns round caste, the Buddha points out that the so-called purity of his ancestry was a myth: 'If one were to follow up your ancient name and lineage' says the Buddha, 'on the father's and mother's side it would appear that one of your ancestors was the offspring of one of the slave girls of the Sakyas.'[2] Later Buddhist polemics against caste continue such arguments. Asvaghosa says: 'Do you say that he who is sprung from Brahmin parents is a Brahmin? Still I object that, since you must mean pure and true Brahmins, in such case the breed of Brahmins must be at an end; since the fathers of the parent race of Brahmins are not, any of them, free from the suspicion of having wives who notoriously commit adultery with Sudras. Now, if the real father be a Sudra, the son cannot be a Brahmin, notwithstanding the Brahminhood of his mother.'[3]

Although the physical constitution of the child is held to be due to a combination of genetical factors derived from both parents, it is important to note that the pre-natal growth of the child takes place, according to Buddhism, in conjunction with the psychic factor constituting the impressions of former births, so that in addition to the effects of biological heredity and environment there is the influence of the psychic factor on the development of the personality. This fact is also made use of by means of a *reductio ad absurdum* to argue against the reality of caste. It is said that the psychic factor or the spirit seeking rebirth (*gandabbho*) cannot be considered as belonging to any particular caste,[4] so that the essence of one's personality is beyond caste distinctions.

---

1. D. I.
2. D. I. 92.
3. H. H. Wilson, op. cit., p. 298.
4. M. II. 157.

44

Another way of combating caste theory revolves round the investigation of the nature and origins of human society and of caste divisions.

The Hindu conception of society was static and was dominated by the idea of caste. The traditional fourfold order of priests, soldiers and administrators, merchants and agriculturists and menial workers was considered not only to be absolute, fundamental and necessary to society but was also given a divine sanction by being considered a creation of God (Brahma). 'God created the fourfold caste order with their specific aptitudes and functions', with the result that people born into the different castes have certain special biologically inherited aptitudes which eminently fit them to perform the caste functions which it is their duty to perform.

Against this was the dynamic evolutionary conception of society as pictured in Early Buddhism. The fourfold order is here not considered absolute since, as the Buddha says, in certain societies there are only two classes (*dve'va vaṇṇā*)— the lords and the serfs or the masters and the slaves, and that not too rigid a division since 'the masters sometimes become slaves and the slaves masters'.[1] Nor is caste divine in origin. The belief that caste was a creation of God and that the Brahmins were the chosen legitimate children of God, 'born of the mouth of Brahma', a conception which is as old as the Rigveda, is denied in the Buddhist texts where it is said that the birth of Brahmins, as is well known, is in no way different from that of other human beings,[2] and the Brahmins are referred to ironically as 'the kinsmen of God' (*brahma-bandhu*). In place of this conception of a divinely ordained fourfold order, Buddhism conceived of caste divisions as being occupational divisions which arose owing to historical circumstances and considered the perpetuation of caste prejudice and discrimination as being due largely to the sanctions given it by the early Brahmin priesthood.

This is well brought out in the story of Devala the Dark, a well-known priest himself, who was scorned because of his colour by the other priestly seers who are said, in the words of the Buddha, to have got together and formulated the

---

1. ibid.
2. M. II. 149.

following *false and evil view* (*pāpakam diṭṭhigatam*), namely that 'the Brahmins were the highest caste while the others were low caste, the Brahmins were the "whites" while the others were "blacks", the Brahmins alone were saved while the others were not, and the Brahmins alone were the only chosen legitimate children of God'.[1] If this legend contains a germ of historical truth, then in the words of Ghurye[2] 'caste in India must be regarded as a Brahmanic child of the Indo-Aryan culture, cradled in the land of the Ganges and thence transferred to the other parts of India by the Brahmin-prospectors'.

In place of a static conception of a fourfold order created by God, a Buddhist myth genesis (found in the texts of both schools of Buddhism) gives an evolutionary account of society and shows how what later became caste divisions arose from a necessary division of functions in society at a certain stage of social evolution. To quote from Professor Rhys Davids' brief summary of the myth: 'Then successively fine moss, and sweet creepers, and delicate rice appeared, and each time the beings ate thereof with a similar result. Then differences of sex appeared; and households were formed; and the lazy stored up the rice, instead of gathering it each evening and morning; and the rights of property arose, and were infringed. And when lusts were felt and thefts committed the beings, now become men, met together, and chose men differing from the others in no wise except in virtue (*dhamma*), to restrain the evildoers by blame or fines or banishment. These were the first Kshatriyas. And others they chose to restrain the evil dispositions which led to the evil-doing. And these were the first Brahmins, differing from the others in no wise, except only in virtue (*dhamma*). Then certain others, to keep their households going, and maintain their wives, started occupations of various kinds. And these were the first Vessas. And some abandoned their homes and became the first recluses (*samanas*). But all were alike in origin, and the only distinction between them was in virtue.'[3] As Professor Rhys Davids comments, 'We may not accept the historical accuracy of this legend. Indeed a continual note of good-humoured irony runs through the whole story.... But it reveals a sound and healthy insight and is much nearer to

---

1. M. II. 156.
2. op. cit., p. 143.
3. 'Dialogues of the Buddha', Part I, *Sacred Books of the Buddhists*, Vol. II, p. 106.

the actual facts than the Brahmin legend it was intended to replace.'[1]

The Buddhist texts constantly refer to the theory of caste which the Brahmin priesthood tried to impose on society—justifying on religious grounds and attempting to perpetuate caste prejudice and discrimination—as a mere propagandist cry (*ghoso*)[2] on their part. Such propaganda was met by the Buddhists by appealing to the historical facts about the origins of caste which gave no basis for the rigidity of caste structure or for prejudice and discrimination between castes, since caste names were in origin and even in the time of the Buddha designations denoting differences of occupation.

It has been argued with some justification that the social organization of eastern India was possibly different from the west where Brahminism held sway.[3] But from the Brahmanical works it is evident that theory was different from practice even in regions where Brahminism held sway, for we find that although certain restricted duties and occupations were considered to be suitable for Brahmins, in actual fact the professions of Brahmins were multifarious and there were among them not only tradesmen and military advisers but even butchers and carriers of corpses, professions which were being confined to the Sudras in the laws drawn up by the Brahmin priests.[4]

In the circumstances, the Buddhists tried to uphold the cause of the social equality of man, illustrating their case against the Brahmanical attack by pointing to actual conditions prevailing in the society of the time. They pointed out that the ability to command the services and labour of others depended not on one's caste or high birth, which *ipso facto* made the Brahmins or the Ksatriyas the masters, but on the wealth that one had. A Sudra who could command enough wealth could easily have a Brahmin or Ksatriya servant to attend to him and be a menial in his household.[5] There was no intrinsic reason why a Sudra should be born to serve others, since in society it was economic power that counted and not caste superiority in requisitioning the services of others. It was shown that all were in fact, and should be, equal be-

---

1. ibid.
2. M. I. 89.
3. R. Fick, *The Social Organization in North-East India in Buddha's Time* (trans. by S. Maitra, Calcutta, 1920), p. 13 ff.
4. 'Laws of Manu', *Sacred Books of the East*, Vol. XXV, III. 150-68.
5. M. II. 85.

fore the law. Even the Laws of Manu,[1] speak of 'Brahmins who are thieves and outcasts' and who on this account lose their right to be Brahmins. This shows that, even where Brahminism held sway, to some extent at least it was their deeds and not birth that mattered. In the Buddhist texts, however, it is said that such robbers, irrespective of whether they were born of Brahmin or Sudra parents, were executed, burnt or exiled by the king quite regardless of their pedigree.[2]

Although Brahmins were denying the Sudras admission into their religious orders, and even the possibility of salvation or moral development, on the grounds that Sudras were born to serve and their nature was untruth itself, non-Brahmanic religious orders represented by the Samanas (the Garmanes of Megasthenes) admitted people of all castes,[3] even the Sudras, and it is said that such people were honoured as 'religieux' even by the kings.[4] In contrast to the Brahmins, who were trying to make a monopoly of religion, the Buddhists idealize a society in which all men irrespective of their social standing or birth were free to join religious orders and receive equal recognition as men of religion.

While the Brahmins argued that only people of the different castes were capable of or suitable for performing certain functions which were considered to be obligatory on their part by virtue of their birth, the Buddhists tried to show that this was by no means so. It is said, for instance, not without some sarcasm that people of all castes whether 'high' or 'low' are capable of kindling a fire and that a fire that men of the so-called 'low' castes would kindle would be no less bright than the fires kindled by the so-called 'higher' castes.[5] The choice of 'kindling a fire' as the example is probably an ironical reference to the Brahmins, who specialized in the kindling and tending of sacrificial fires.

The hollowness of the magical notions associated with the concept of caste pollution is exposed by the empiricist stand of Buddhism. The only sense of cleanliness or pollution, barring the spiritual sense (see below), was the physical sense and it is said with biting irony that people of all 'castes' even the Sudras can soap themselves and bathe in the river

---

1. III. 150.
2. M. II. 88.
3. J. III. 381; IV. 392.
4. M. II. 89.
5. M. II. 151, 152.

48

and be equally clean,[1] so that Sudras are not at a disadvantage in their ability to be clean.

Thus, according to Buddhism all men, irrespective of their caste or race, had equal rights and deserved equal opportunities for development as members of a single social order which embraced a common humanity. It was a man's social status as determined by the wealth that he possessed, and not his birth in a particular caste or racial group, which made it possible for him to command the services of others whatever their pedigree might be. All men likewise, irrespective of race or caste, should be equal before the law. The aptitudes of people do not depend on their birth in a particular caste or race. The moral worth of a person should receive social recognition regardless of the caste to which he belonged and all men should receive equal opportunity for moral and spiritual development since all men were capable of it.

It was in these terms that Buddhism proclaimed the equality of man as a member of human society. The constant refrain that we find in these discussions, which are intended to counter the Brahmin claims to superiority by virtue of their birth, is that considering the capabilities of men of all castes 'people of all castes are on an equal footing' (*evam sante ime cattaro vanna samasama honti*), and that 'there is no distinction whatsoever among them in these respects' (*na'sam ettha kinci nānākaranam samanupassāmi*).[2]

Ethical and Religious Arguments

As mentioned above, Buddhism denied in the light of historical facts the special prerogatives that the Brahmins claimed in matters of religion. Their claim to be the chosen children of God by virtue of their birth and their exclusive claim to salvation were shown to be false, since people of all castes, given the opportunity, were capable of attaining the spiritual heights required for salvation. In place of the Brahmin claim that 'Brahmins alone were saved and not others', we find it stated in the words of the Brahmin opponents of Buddhism that the 'recluse Gotama proclaims the possibility of salvation to all men of all four castes' (*Samano*

---

1. M. II. 151.
2. M. I. 85-9.

Gotama catuvannim suddhim pannapeti). [1] All men irrespective of caste were capable of spiritual development, and a man whether born in a 'high' caste or 'low' 'can develop within him loving thoughts towards all beings'. [2] Such religious exercises were within the capacity of all and make for their spiritual progress. Similarly the claim to a divine origin for caste was condemned as mere propaganda on the part of the Brahmin priests and as having no basis in view of the gradual evolutionary origins of society.

All men are likewise equal before the moral law. Men are judged in the hereafter by the good and evil they do, and not by the stations of life in which they were placed by virtue of their birth. The reward and punishment are strictly in proportion to the good and evil done, and caste whether 'high' or 'low' does not matter in the least. A Sudra (outcast) who does good in this humble station enjoys later the pleasant fruits of his actions, while a Brahmin who does evil suffers. The magical concept of cleanliness and pollution associated with caste is given an ethical twist; what matters is not even external cleanliness but purity of heart or the absence of pollution within. [3] Moral and spiritual development is not a prerogative of people who are specially favoured by their birth, but is open to all and is within the reach of all.

THE SPIRITUAL UNITY OF MANKIND

Biologically man was one species. As members of a common human society all men deserved to have equal rights and opportunities, which included the opportunities for moral and spiritual development. But man was more than a biological specimen or a social being. Deep within his desires to satisfy his biological needs and social instincts was his quest for security, immortality and a lasting peace and happiness.

What brought men together was the realization of their common lot and their common humanity. All men of whatever race were subject to disease, decay and death. All men were likewise impelled by the desires within them—the desire for sense-gratification, the desire for life or personal immortality, and the desire for domination over death.

---

1. M. II. 147.
2. M. II. 151.
3. Sn, 43.

50

Man's quest for security and lasting happiness never ceases, but it is never satisfied by pandering to his desires as a result of which he is continually in a state of unrest. But deep within this fathom-long body, says the Buddha, is the final goal we all seek and it is only by discovering this eternal peace and happiness within us that we realize the highest that we are capable of.

All people, whatever their caste or racial origins may be, are in need of and capable of this self-same salvation. The King of Kosala once questioned the Buddha on this subject: 'There are these four castes, Sir—Ksatriyas, Brahmins, Vaisyas and Sudras. Let us suppose them to be imbued with the five forms of strenuous exertion to attain salvation. In this case would there be any distinction, Sir, any difference between them [in regard to the quality of their salvation]?'

'Here, too, Sire,' replies the Buddha, 'I do not admit any difference whatsoever in regard to the nature of their salvation. Just as if, Sire, a man were to kindle a fire with dry herbs, and another man were to kindle a fire with dry sal-wood, and a third were to kindle a fire with dry mango-wood, and a fourth with dry fig-wood—what think you, Sire? Would these diverse fires kindled with diverse woods show any difference whatsoever in respect of their flame, hue or brightness?'

'No difference at all, Sir.'

'Even so, Sire, is the inward illumination which is kindled by effort and nursed by strenuous exertion. I say that there is no difference whatsoever herein in regard to their salvation.'[1]

All men have the capacity to attain salvation, irrespective of the race or caste to which they belong, and it is this quest for eternal happiness which constitutes the religious quest of man.

It is the realization of this quest which should be the ultimate aim of man, for it is only on attaining it that his mental conflicts are at an end and he has found salvation, a state to be attained in this life itself and not necessarily in the hereafter. 'Man', says the Buddha, 'is subject to both bodily and mental disease. Bodily disease afflicts him only from time to time, but except for those who have attained salvation the others cannot claim to have perfect mental

---

1. M. II. 129, 130.

health even for a second.'[1] But such perfect control and poise of mind which awakens in us a peace that passeth understanding can only be found by those who practise love and charity to all beings and engage in the development of their minds by following the process of self-analysis as recommended in Buddhism. And being obsessed by one's 'superior' birth in respect of the race or caste to which one belongs is one of the first obstacles that has to be put away in the interests of our own mental health as well as of the world. The outcast as described in Buddhism is not one who is born in a particular caste but 'one who hardens his heart by virtue of his birth in a particular race (*jati-tthaddho*), or by virtue of his wealth (*dhana-tthaddho*) or caste (*gotta-tthaddho*), and despises his neighbour (*sam ñātim atimaññeti*)'.[2]

So when we consider differences among human beings it is not the shape of their limbs, the colour of their skins, their parentage or social status that matters, but the question how far each human being is from his goal, which is also the goal of all mankind, and which gives him real happiness and perfect mental health. Are we progressing towards this goal or away from it? It is solely in virtue of the degree of moral and spiritual attainment of people, irrespective of race or caste, that Buddhism classified human beings as superior or inferior—although this classification too is not rigid inasmuch as each person is constantly changing and has within himself the power to change for better or for worse. The superior ones are those who have attained the goal or are near it or are progressing towards it, while the inferior ones are those who are far from the goal or are going away from it. And significantly enough it is said that those who are 'bound by racial prejudices' (*jati-vada-vinibaddha*) or 'bound by caste prejudices' (*gotta-vada-vinibaddha*) have strayed 'far from the way of salvation' (*araka anuttaraya vijja-carana-sampadaya*).[3]

It is also a characteristic of the superior ones that they do not assert or make personal claims of their moral and spiritual superiority over others.[4] This does not however mean that they are conscious of their superiority but merely do not show it, for it is said that those who have attained salvation cease to think of themselves in terms of 'being superior'

---

1. A. II. 143.
2 ' Sn. 104.
3. D. I. 99.
4. Sn. 782, 918.

52

(*seyyo*), 'being inferior' (*niceyyo*) or 'being equal' (*sarikkho*).[1]
The morally and spiritually inferior ones on the other hand
shut their minds to the possibility of a spiritual awakening
and cease to make any moral or spiritual progress as a result
of their asserting or claiming superiority over their fellow
beings on baseless grounds, and thus bringing unhappiness
both on themselves and on others by causing baseless divisions among men. The degree of moral and spiritual progress
is therefore the only criterion by which men should be
classified as being superior or inferior—though such classifications are not absolute since men are changing and can
change.

Thus we have no right to despise another. Even a hardened
criminal like Angulimala, the outcast robber, who was converted by the Buddha, may have deep within his nature strong
potentialities for undergoing a relatively quick spiritual
transformation. The truly superior being is never conscious
of his superiority, nor does he claim it. Such people are the
true Brahmins, regardless of their origins, and not those who
are obsessed by their claims to a 'pure' birth.

There are several such classifications of mankind on the
basis of their varying moral and spiritual attainments in the
Buddhist texts. We may refer to one which classifies individuals into seven grades:

'There are these seven persons to be compared with those
immersed in water, viz., one who is once drowned is drowned,
one who is drowned after emergence, etc. . . .

'(1) How is a person who is once drowned just drowned?
Here a certain person is possessed of absolutely black immoral qualities. Such a person being once drowned is drowned.

'(2) How is a person drowned after emergence? Here a
certain person emerges with faith, with modesty, with conscientiousness, with energy, with insight, as regards good
(moral) qualities, but his faith, his modesty, conscientiousness,
energy or insight neither persists nor grows, but decreases.
Such a person is drowned after emergence.

'(3) How does a person persist after emergence? Here
a certain person emerges with faith, with modesty, with
conscientiousness, with energy, with insight, as regards good
qualities and his faith, his modesty, conscientiousness, energy,
or insight neither decreases nor grows, but persists. Such a
person persists after emergence.

---

1. Sn. 918.

'(4) How does a person look about and around after emergence? Here a certain person emerges with faith, with modesty, with conscientiousness, with energy, or with insight, as regards good qualities. By complete destruction of three fetters he becomes a stream-attainer, no more liable to fall into a woeful state, but sure to win enlightenment as his final end and aim. Such a person looks about and around after emergence.

'(5) How does a person swim on after emergence? Here a certain person emerges with faith, with modesty, with conscientiousness, with energy, or with insight, as regards good qualities. By complete destruction of three fetters and by the destruction of passion, hatred, and delusion he becomes a once-returner, who coming back but once to this world makes an end of suffering. Such a person swims on after emergence.

'(6) How does a person reach a fixed footing after emergence? Here a certain person emerges with faith, with modesty, with conscientiousness, with energy or with insight, as regards good qualities. By complete destruction of five fetters causing rebirth in the lower worlds, he becomes a being of apparitional rebirth attaining the final release in that state, and is not liable to return from that world. Such a person reaches a fixed footing after emergence.

'(7) What sort of person is he who as a true Brahmin after emergence crosses to the other shore and establishes himself in fruition? Here a certain person emerges with faith, with modesty, with conscientiousness, with energy or with insight, as regards good qualities. By destruction of sinful tendencies, he lives in possession of emancipation of will, of emancipation of insight, free from those sinful tendencies and having come to know and realize them by his own efforts in this very existence. Such a person is a true Brahmin crossing after emergence and going to the other shore and establishing himself in fruition.'[1]

---

1. *Human Types* (trans. by B. C. Law, Pali Text Society, 1924), pp. 99, 100.

THE PRACTICAL POLICY OF BUDDHISM TOWARDS RACISM AND CASTE

As we tried to show in the previous chapter, Buddhism from the first proclaimed the oneness of mankind and denied that birth in a particular race or caste was or should be an obstacle towards anyone developing his potentialities as a man or as a spiritual being. 'Race' names and 'caste' names were convenient if misleading designations, but they were not absolute divisions. Caste names had only an occupational significance and from what appears in the texts the people at that time were still relatively free to choose or change their occupations. Caste prejudice and discrimination were still in the formative stage; their foundations were being laid by the Brahmin priesthood who were formulating the required religious and legal sanctions for perpetuating the system. In the circumstances, we find the Buddha and his disciples completely ignoring the claims attached to birth with regard to dispensation of the Order of Monks—while fighting caste prejudice and discrimination, fanned by the Brahmin priesthood in the prevalent social order, by the methods of rational persuasion and example.

As Professor Rhys Davids says, the Buddha 'ignores completely and absolutely all advantages or disadvantages arising from birth, occupation or social status and sweeps away all barriers and disabilities arising from the arbitrary rules of mere ceremonial or social impurity'.[1] People of all castes were freely admitted to the order and in doing so people had to change even their names and designations because of their associations with their rank or birth. There were possibly a few who while being members of the Order of Monks were still conscious of their 'high' birth or lineage and tried to claim special privileges on these grounds but such attempts were always checked and sternly denounced. It is said that a section of such monks who were conscious of their 'high' rank as civilians tried to monopolize lodgings,

---

1. 'Dialogues of the Buddha', Part I, *Sacred Books of the Buddhists*, Vol. I, p. 100.

thereby leaving out the senior elders of the Order. The Buddha inquiring into the matter asked them, 'Tell me, who deserves the best lodging, the best water, and the best rice, brethren?' Whereupon some answered 'He who was a nobleman before he became a brother', and others said, 'He who was originally a Brahmin, or a man of means.' The Buddha's reply was: 'In the religion which I teach, the standard by which precedence in the matter of lodging and the like is to be settled, is not noble birth, or having been a Brahmin, or having been wealthy before entry into the Order. . . .'[1]

Some of the most distinguished members of the Order were from the so-called 'low' castes. Upali, who was the chief authority on the rules of the Order after Buddha himself, had formerly been a barber, one of the despised occupations of the 'lower' castes. Punna and Punnikā, who joined the Order of Nuns had been slave girls. The members of the Order, whether male or female, do not seem however to have been drawn exclusively from the 'lower' castes. An analysis of the social position of the nuns mentioned in the *Psalms of the Sisters* shows that 8½ per cent of the whole number were 'base-born'.[2] Professor Rhys Davids says: 'It is most likely that this is just about the proportion which persons in similar social rank bore to the rest of the population.'[2] Perhaps it would be nearer the truth to say that if 8½ per cent of the contributed poems were composed by and express the religious joy that the members of the despised castes felt on joining the Order and realizing the fruits of the training that it gave, then the actual percentage of the women of 'low' birth in the Order would have been very much larger, since the social class from which they were drawn was mostly illiterate. As Mrs. Rhys Davids says in the introduction to the sister work, the *Psalms of the Brethren*: 'That a large proportion of these men of "letters" should belong to the class who were the custodians of religious lore and sacred hymns was inevitable. The really interesting feature is that the residuum, consisting of noblemen trained in war, governance, and sports, of merchants, craftsmen, and the like, occupied with business, commerce and constructive work, and of the illiterate poor, should be as numerous as it is. Or, indeed, that there should have been any of the last-named group at all as composers of verses deserving inclusion in the Canon. In

---

1. *The Jataka* (trans.), Vol. I, pp. 92, 93.
2. op. cit., p. 102.

56

fact, it would not be entirely unreasonable to conclude that if 4 per cent of the canonical poets were drawn from the poor and despised of the earth, from whom no such products as verses could be expected, then the proportion of monks, *in general,* coming from that class may have been considerable.' [1]

How the Buddha called men and women from the lowliest walks of life and made them realize the richness of their spiritual heritage as human beings even though they were despised and reckoned as only fit for menial work by some of their fellow men—who ought to have known better—is best described in the words of those who received such gifts not as a matter of grace but as a fruit of their own efforts. Sunita, for example, was a scavenger and the following is a brief account of his life and successful quest told in verse in his own words:

> Humble the clan wherein I took my birth,
> And poor was I and scanty was my lot;
> Mean task was mine, a scavenger of flowers,
> One for whom no man cared, despised, abused,
> My mind I humbled and I bent the head
> In deference to a goodly tale of folk.
> And then I saw the All-Enlightened come,
> Begirt and followed by his bhikkhu-train,
> Great Champion ent'ring Magadha's chief town.
> I laid aside my baskets and my yoke,
> And came where I might due obeisance make,
> And of his loving kindness just for me,
> The Chief of men halted upon his way.
> Low at his feet I bent, then standing by,
> I begged the Master's leave to join the Rule
> And follow him, of every creature Chief.
> Then he whose tender mercy watcheth all
> The world, the Master pitiful and kind,
> Gave me my answer: 'Come, Bhikkhu!' he said
> Thereby to me was ordination given.
>
> Lo! I alone in forest depths abode,
> With zeal unfaltering wrought the Master's word,
> Even the counsels of the Conqueror.
> While passed the first watch of the night there rose
> Long memories of the bygone line of lives.
> While passed the middle watch, the heav'nly eye,
> Purview celestial, was clarified.

---

1. *Psalms of the Brethren* (Pali Text Society), p. xxix.

While passed the last watch of the night, I burst
Asunder all the gloom of ignorance.
Then as night wore down at dawn
And rose the sun, came Indra and Brahma,
Yielding me homage with their clasped hands:
Hail unto thee, thou nobly born of men!
Hail unto thee, thou highest among men!
Perished for thee are all th'intoxicants;
And thou art worthy, noble sir, of gifts.

The Master, seeing me by troop of gods
Begirt and followed, thereupon a smile
Revealing by his utterance made response;
'By discipline of holy life, restraint
And mastery of self : hereby a man
Is holy; this is holiness supreme!'[1]

It was the same with the women. To quote a few extracts from the utterances of Punna, who was once a slave girl:

Drawer of water, I down to the stream,
Even in winter went in fear of blows,
Harassed by fear of blame from mistress...
. . . .
Lo! to the Buddha I for refuge go,
And to the Norm and Order. I will learn
Of them to take upon my self and keep
The Precepts; so shall I indeed find good.

Once a son of Brahmins born was I,
Today I stand Brahmin in every deed.
The nobler Threefold Wisdom[2] have I won,
Won the true Veda-lore, and graduate
Am I, from better Sacrament returned,
Cleansed by the inward spiritual bath.[3]

The training for realizing their spiritual potentialities which they received as members of the Order was such that not only did race or caste consciousness have no place in it but such prejudices actually hindered the awakening of spiritual insight and the cultivation of the moral life. As we said before, 'Those who are obsessed with the prejudices of

---

1. ibid., p. 273.
2. i.e. (i) the faculty of seeing one's past births, (ii) clairvoyance and (iii) the knowledge of one's inner mental processes.
3. *Psalms of the Sisters* (Pali Text Society), pp. 117-19.

58

race or caste are far from the moral life and the attainment
of supreme spiritual insight.' Such obsessions, which are the
accumulated products of acquired erroneous beliefs, are
among the intoxicants (*avijjâsava*) of the mind and have to
be got rid of by a process of self-analysis and conscious elimi-
nation. 'Intoxicants are to be eliminated by seeing and
recognizing them as they affect our mind and not by being
blind to them.'[1] This requires watchfulness (*sati*) on our
part, the acquiring of right views (*dassanā*) to replace the
erroneous ones, constant vigilance over our thoughts (*samvara*)
and the cultivation of our mind (*bhāvanā*). The practice of
mettā or compassion towards all beings, and of *upekkhā* or
equanimity or impartiality towards all, would be considered
impossible on the part of those who have not freed their
minds of the initial prejudices associated with race or caste.

How Buddhism set about to explode the theory of caste
by adducing historical, scientific, ethical and religious arguments against it we have mentioned already. If we consider
these arguments we see that they do not merely represent a
trend of Ksatriya opposition to Brahmin claims to superiority
for it is constantly pointed out that men of all castes are on
an equal footing (*samasama*) with regard to their capabilities,
and the Ksatriya and Vaisya claims to superiority are as
much denounced in this respect as those of the Brahmins.
There is however one statement which in the opinion of the
authors has sometimes been misinterpreted to mean that
Buddhism championed the cause of the superiority of the
Ksatriyas over the Brahmins and all else. It occurs in a
discourse against caste which ends on the theme that what
really matters is moral superiority and not the pretensions
of 'high' birth. 'The Ksatriya is the best of those among his
folk who put their trust in lineage. But he who is perfect
in wisdom and righteousness, he is the best among gods and
men.'[2] It would of course be possible to explain this text
away by attributing it to the work of some of the editors of
the Canon who were unconsciously influenced by notions of
superiority based on birth, but this would be unnecessary if
the statement is carefully studied in its context. It would
then be seen that what the Buddha does in this discourse is
to employ a dialectical method of argument whereby he takes
up some of the criteria which the Brahmins (he is arguing

---

1. M. I. 7.
2. D. I. 99.

with a Brahmin) accept as proof of caste superiority and showing that when they are actually applied to the context of society it would show the superiority of the Ksatriya and not the Brahmin—thus proving that the Brahmin claim to superiority in respect of these criteria was baseless. Lineage is of little or no account but if lineage (as defined here) is taken as the criterion then it is the Ksatriya who should claim superiority and not the Brahmin. The fact that, as Hutton says, 'the Brahmin in the Rigveda seems to have been second in social importance to the Rajanya'[1] lends historical support to this deduction. In any case the point of this quotation is that he who is supreme above all is the one 'who is perfect in wisdom and righteousness', a supremacy not based on the claims of birth.

The attempt at influencing public opinion by rational persuasion and example was not backed up merely by the exemplary organization of the Buddhist Order of monks and nuns, who did away with all distinctions or claims based on birth. The monks and nuns visited the homes of people of all castes, 'high' or 'low', for purposes of preaching and having their meals, sometimes at the cost of personal discomfort. The Buddha was sometimes railed at by Brahmins for visiting their homes to beg for meals and his invariable answer as to what was his race or caste was 'Ask me not for my birth' (*ma jātim puccha*).[2] Sometimes he visited Brahmin villages without getting a morsel of food. The disciples did the same, and ignored caste distinctions and practices in their relations with their fellow human beings. The following incident is recorded of Ananda, one of the immediate disciples of the Buddha, who rehearsed the dharma at the first Council: 'Now the elder Ananda dressed early and taking his bowl and robe entered the great city of Sravasti for alms. After his round and having finished his meal he approached a certain well. At that time a Matanga (outcast) girl named Prakrti was at the well drawing water. So the elder Ananda said to the Matanga girl, 'Give me water, sister, I wish to drink.' At this she replied 'I am a Matanga girl, reverend Ananda.' 'I do not ask you, sister, about your family or caste but if you have any water left over, give it me, I wish to drink.' Then she gave Ananda the water....[3]

---

1. Hutton, op. cit., p. 156.
2. Sn. 462.
3. Divyavadana, p. 611 ff., quoted in E. J. Thomas, *The Life of Buddha*, p. 242.

It is not only the monks and nuns who have to practise compassion but the lay disciples as well. The following are among the sentiments expressed in stanzas recited frequently by lay Buddhists even today:

'Whatever living beings there are, either feeble or strong, all either long or great, middle-sized, short, small or large.

'Either seen or which are not seen, and which live far [or] near, either born or seeking birth, may all creatures be happy-minded.

'Let no one deceive another, let him not despise [another] in any place, let him not out of anger or resentment wish harm to another.

'As a mother at the risk of her life watches over her own child, her only child, so also let everyone cultivate a boundless [friendly] mind towards all beings.'[1]

The cultivation of such sentiments is incompatible with the harbouring of any racial prejudice or hatred. Lay disciples were admonished to give up conceit based on notions of 'high' birth, or in other words racial or caste pride. In a sermon which distinguishes between the characteristics of the man who progresses and the man who degenerates, this is reckoned among one of the many causes for the downfall of man: 'The man who, proud of his birth, wealth or family, despises his neighbour is degenerate',[2] and this conceit would be the cause of his downfall. It is also not surprising that among the trades forbidden to Buddhists is the slave trade or 'trafficking in human beings' (*satta-vanijjā*)[3] as this would not be in keeping with 'the right mode of livelihood' (*sammā ājīva*) which every Buddhist must follow. The treatment of the servants in one's household too should be such that their human dignity is recognized. 'They should not be over-burdened with work, they should be well provided with their meals and wages, they should be looked after when they are ill, the food and delicacies should be shared with them and they should be given enough leave and leisure.'[4] Thus did Buddhism lighten the lot of a class of people who were considered to have been born or created to serve their masters and to be expelled at will (*kāmotthāpyah*) or to be slain at will (*yathākāmavaddhyah*), according to the texts of the Brahmins.

---

1. *Sacred Books of the East*, Vol. X, p. 25.
2. Sn. 104.
3. A. III. 308.
4. D. III. 191.

It was in keeping with these Buddhist ideals and principles that in the third century B.C. the great Buddhist emperor Asoka modelled his policy towards the lower strata of society in his kingdom, the subject races, the forest tribes and the border peoples. Quoting the Buddhist saying that the 'gift of the Dharma excels all other gifts' we find his Rock Edict XII calling attention before all else to the just treatment of servants and slaves: 'There is no gift that can equal in merit the gift of Dharma.... From it follow the right treatment of slaves and servants, service to mother and father....'[1] And what he preached he seemed to have practised himself to judge by the record of his inscriptions·

Believing in the equality of man as an adherent of the Dharma he seems to have treated his subjects, irrespective of race or social status, equally before the law, notwithstanding what was prescribed in Hindu legal codes. 'It is most desirable' he says in Pillar Edict IV, 'that there should be absolute equality for all in all legal proceedings and in the punishments awarded....'[2] He extends this equality of treatment even to the border tribes, in Kalinga Edict II making the following declaration: 'All people are my children. Just as I desire, on behalf of my own children, that they should be fully provided with all kinds of comfort and enjoyment in this world as well as in the other world, similarly I desire the same on behalf of all people. Those who live on the borders of my dominions, and have not been conquered by me, may wonder what exactly is my disposition towards them. My disposition towards them is this: they should be told that the King desires thus: "Let them not be afraid of me. Let them be made to feel confident that they need expect only happiness from me and not misery." They should again be told thus: "The King will forgive their faults that can be forgiven. May they be induced to practise Dharma for my sake and thereby attain happiness in this world and in the next."... Your action should be shaped accordingly and the borderers should be comforted and consoled and inspired with confidence and with this idea: "The King is like our father. He cares for our welfare as much as he cares for himself. We are to him, like his own children".[3] In the Ninth Rock Edict (Girnar) Asoka recommends the practice

---

1. *Edicts of Asoka (Adyar Library Series)*, p. 33.
2. ibid., p. 95.
3. ibid., pp. 62, 63, 65.

of the law of piety and discourages vain ritual and ceremonies, which possibly included the practice of caste rites: 'Men are practising various ceremonies during illness or at the marriage of a son or daughter, or at the birth of a son, or when setting out on a journey; on these and other occasions men are practising various ceremonies. And women are practising many and various vulgar and useless ceremonies. Now, ceremonies should certainly be practised. But ceremonies like these bear little fruit indeed. But the following practice bears much fruit, namely, the practice of morality. Herein the following [are comprised]: proper courtesy to slaves and servants, reverence to elders, gentleness to animals....'[1] He proclaims that those of the humblest origins, even among the border tribes, are capable of experiencing the highest spiritual joy and in the Brahmagiri and Rupnath Edicts he enjoins his people to exert themselves in this direction: 'Men in Jambudipa, who were till now unmingled, have now been mingled with the gods. This is certainly the fruit of my exertion. Nor is it correct to hold that this can be achieved only by the great ones, for even the smallest person can achieve the ideal of heavenly bliss by force of exertion. It is for this purpose that this proclamation has been proclaimed thus: "Let the humble and the great exert themselves to achieve this ideal. May my border people understand this. May this spirit of exertion endure everlastingly." '[2]

The care and concern with which he referred to the weaker aboriginal tribes dwelling in the hills and borderlands of his territory, was indeed enlightened beyond much modern practice. He regarded them not as savage beasts who deserved to be exterminated or as fierce peoples who should be kept in check by the fear and force of arms but as human children who were to be made to understand that they were under his care and protection. In Rock Edict XIII he says: 'Devanampriya considers that even he who wrongs him is fit to be forgiven of wrongs that can be forgiven. And even the forest inhabitants included in the dominions of Devanampriya, who submit, he pacifies and converts [by kindly methods], duly informing them of his power to punish them, in spite of his compassion. And what for? In order that they may feel ashamed of their past conduct, and not be killed. Because Devanampriya desires that all beings should

---

1. Hultzsch, *Corpus Inscriptionum Indicarum*, Vol. I, pp. 112, 113.
2. op. cit., 70, 71.

be left unhurt, should have self-control, have equal [impartial] treatment and should lead happy lives.'[1]

Buddhism was from the first a missionary religion which sought to bring the message of truth and love to all mankind. 'Go ye forth,' said the Buddha to his disciples, 'I am delivered from all fetters, human and divine. Ye are also delivered from all fetters human and divine. Go ye now and wander for the gain of the many, for the welfare of the many, out of compassion for the world, for the good, for the gain, and for the welfare of gods and men. Let not two of you go the same way.'[2] And they were to go, as they did go, to all manners of peoples and tribes, regardless of the hazards of such journeys and the dangers of trying to understand and convert strange peoples. Yet the only weapons they were allowed to take and have with them were the weapons of truth and love. Their training in the practice of compassion should be such that, in the words of the Buddha, 'they would not have done his bidding if they were to manifest the slightest irritation or anger even if wily robbers were to get hold of them on the way and cut them limb by limb with a double-edged saw'.[3] The Buddha's interrogation of Punna just before she set out on such a dangerous mission which however achieved amazing success was as follows:

'With this concise teaching from me, Punna, in what country will you take up your abode?'

'In Sunaparanta, sir.'

'They are a fierce and violent race, Punna, in Sunaparanta. If they were to abuse you and revile you there, what would you think?'

'I should think, Lord, that the good folk of Sunaparanta were really nice people, very nice people indeed, in that they forbore to strike me.'

'But if they strike you?'

'I should think, Lord, that the good folk of Sunaparanta were really nice people ... if they forbore to pelt me with clods.'

'But if they pelt you with clods?'

'I should think, Lord, ... forbore to cudgel me.'

'But if they cudgel you?'

'I should think, Lord, ... forbore to knife me.'

---

1. ibid., pp. 44, 45.
2. *Vinaya Texts* (Oxford, 1881), Part I, pp. 112-13.
3. M. I. 129.

64

'But if they knife you?'
'I should think, Lord, ... forbore to take my life.'
'But if they take your life?'
'If they did, Lord, I should think that there are disciples
of the Lord, who in their tribulation and despair, are on the
look-out for someone with a knife, and that I have found
him without having to hunt about. This is what I should
think, Lord; that would be my thought, Blessed One.'
'Good indeed, Punna. With such a command of yourself,
you will be able to live with the folk of Sunaparanta.'[1]

How far Buddhism succeeded by these methods of gentle
persuasion and example in stemming the tide of caste in India
is a problem about which we do not wish to be dogmatic for,
especially after the Asokan era, Brahmanism gradually came
back into its own, and with it the sanctions for the hardening
of the caste structure. But if the account of a great Chinese
saint and traveller of the fifth century is to be trusted, on
the whole a Buddhist atmosphere prevailed in India even
then. He says: 'The people are numerous and happy; they
have not to register their households or attend to any magis-
trates or their rules; only those who have to cultivate the
royal land have to pay [a portion of] the gain from it. If
they want to go, they go; if they want to stay, they stay.
The king governs without decapitation or [other] corporal
punishments. Criminals are simply fined, lightly or heavily,
according to the circumstances [of each case]. . . . The king's
bodyguards and attendants all have salaries. . . .'[2] Mention
is however made of the Chandalas, who are fishermen and
hunters, and live apart from the rest of the population, but
this does not necessarily imply the extensive division of the
whole population into numerous castes. Such accounts are
meagre, however, and it is not possible to say how much
caste prejudice and discrimination was present even though
the caste structure was still fairly flexible.

But it is very likely that when the Gita throws open the
road to salvation to all castes this is due to the influence of
Buddhism. Early Brahmanism denied religious instruction
to the Sudras and thought them incapable of salvation, and
in the Buddhist books the Brahmins are quoted as saying
of the Buddha that 'the recluse Gotama proclaims salvation

---

1. *Further Dialogues of the Buddha*, Part II, p. 308.
2. Legge, *A Record of Buddhist Kingdoms*, pp. 42, 43.

to all castes'. Ghurye, following Fick[1] (who only examined part of the material of the Jatakas and left out the major portion of the Canon), holds that 'it is wrong to look upon the Buddha as a social reformer and Buddhism as a revolt against caste',[2] but he grants that 'the actions of Buddha had a general liberalizing effect'[3] and as regards the possibility of salvation for all says that 'the necessity of closing up the ranks against the onslaught of Buddhism and of assuring individual salvation for all led to the formation of two slightly differing philosophies of caste'.[4] It is therefore very likely that, to a great extent at least, the Buddhist movement was responsible in relaxing the rigours of caste in this direction.

Buddhism has spread in many lands and among many races during the 2,500 years of its history, though its light has mainly been confined to the East. The work it did during these years is perhaps partly responsible for knitting these races closely together in one Asian spirit, and in so far as non-aggressiveness and tolerance are to some extent characteristic of this spirit (however dangerous such generalizations may be) they transcend the boundaries of Buddhist lands and embrace the whole earth. This unity is certainly not the unity of orthodox beliefs, for Buddhism never sought to inculcate such orthodoxies and curb the free spirit of inquiry in man. The verdict of one pilgrim traveller in Buddhist lands, Hiuen-Tsiang was: 'In agreement with the mysterious character of this doctrine the world has progressed in its higher destiny; but distant peoples coming to interpret the doctrine, are not in agreement. The time of the Holy One is remote from us, and so the sense of his doctrine is differently expounded. But as the taste of the fruit of different trees of the same kind is the same, so the principles of the schools as they now exist are not different.'[5] This view is reiterated by another such pilgrim of the twentieth century, Pratt, who in his *The Pilgrimage of Buddhism* says: 'Not so obvious, perhaps, are those persistent characteristics which help to make it, in all its ramifications and all its history, still one religion. I shall not, of course, maintain that all those who burn incense in Buddhist temples or employ

---

1. op. cit.
2. op. cit., p. 67.
3. ibid.
4. ibid., p. 60.
5. Beal's translation of *The Life of Hiuen-Tsiang*, p. 31.

Buddhist monks at funerals are Buddhists, any more than I should hold that every ikon-worshipper is necessarily a Christian. What I mean is that there are certain qualities of character and feeling, of point of view, conduct, and belief, which may properly be called Buddhist, and that these are not confined to any one school of Buddhism, whether Hinayana or Mahāyāna, but are to be found in all those who by common consent would be considered typically Buddhist in all the lands we have studied, from southern Ceylon to northern Japan. These qualities, I hold, transcend not only nations but centuries, and unite the earnest follower of the most up-to-date Japanese sect with the earliest disciples of the Founder.'

Pratt adds that 'Taken together, they constitute what, in a rough and general way may be called the Spirit of Buddhism' and goes on to describe that what is particularly characteristic of this spirit is the lack of aggressiveness and the love of life: 'This lack of aggressiveness is one of the most marked of Buddhist traits. . . . There is a kind of gentleness in the Buddhist nature which I think everyone must feel. But this is not the gentleness and non-aggressiveness of weakness. It is not fear that prompts it. . . . The non-aggressiveness of the typical Buddhist is a kind of strength in reserve; it is the gentleness of the strong man who refuses to push his own way in a crowd, or of the reflective man who is convinced the game is not worth the candle. Partly as an outgrowth of this gentleness of spirit, partly in obedience to the never-forgotten exhortations of the Founder, partly out of contagion from the example and influence of his mesmeric personality, Buddhism in all the lands to which it has gone has never ceased to preach and to practise universal pity and sympathy for all sentient life.'

With the exception of Ceylon, where a caste structure prevails side by side very uneasily along with Buddhism, such divisions are wholly absent in Buddhist lands. In fact those who have lived and moved among the peoples in these lands have often been struck by the equality of man in countries steeped in Buddhism and unaffected by the Hindu caste structure. Fielding Hall, writing of the Burmese, says 'There was, and is, absolutely no aristocracy of any kind at all. The Burmese are a community of equals, in a sense that has probably never been known elsewhere.' [1]

---

1. *The Soul of a People* (London, 1903), p. 54.

5*

In Ceylon the proximity of South India was perhaps largely influential in the emergence of a caste structure in society[1] which later became more rigid with the rule of South Indian kings who relied on Hindu legal codes. Yet it is interesting to observe that the classical Sinhalese treatise on caste, the *Janavamsa*, a Sinhalese poem of the fifteenth century, endeavours as Ananda Coomaraswamy says, 'to show that all men are really of one race though occupied in different ways, stress being laid on the well-known saying of the Buddha "not by birth does one become a Vasala [outcast], not by birth does one become a Brahmin...".[2]

The resultant effect of these historical circumstances is a situation which is summed up by Bryce Ryan[3] in the following words. 'Informed Buddhists, of the laity and clergy alike, repudiate sacred foundations for the caste hierarchy. Nor will an ignorant villager, even under the most stringent questioning, admit religious or preceptual basis for the organization of society into castes. The intelligentsia today will relate caste purely to secular foundations, usually noting that such a system is contrary to the Buddha's teaching, and in this context deplore this departure from both the spirit and teachings of the religion. The less sophisticated may not deplore caste organization, but find it from the religious point of view irrelevant. Thus an intelligent villager responds, "Caste is not of the Buddha, it is of the kings." Unlike his educated fellow he is not confronted with the necessity of conventionalizing religious views and secular practices. At no intellectual level do Sinhalese believe that Buddhism supports caste, and in general Western observers have considered the caste system as existing in opposition to religious principles.' In any case the mildness of caste in Ceylon in contrast to what obtains in India is only too apparent. Untouchability is absent, and there is full freedom of worship for people of all castes who sit together in the preaching halls to listen to sermons.

---

1. See Ananda Coomaraswamy, *Medieval Sinhalese Art*, pp. 21 ff.
2. ibid., p. 22.
3. *Caste in Ceylon* (Rutgers Univ. Press, 1953), p. 34.

CONCLUSION

In the foregoing pages we have tried to show that Buddhism
stands for the oneness of the human species, the equality
of man, and the spiritual unity of mankind. The differences
among the so-called races as far as their physical characteristics go are negligible. The differences in cultural attainment are due to historical circumstances and not to any
innate aptitudes with which some of the 'cultured' races,
whether of the East or West, are favoured by nature or God.
All men likewise, irrespective of their race, caste or class,
have the capacity to reach the heights of moral and spiritual
attainment.

Man's destiny is to develop as a spiritual being and therefore what really matters is the degree of his moral and spiritual development. This has no connexion with birth in any
particular race or caste since the 'meanest' and 'humblest'
of mankind may have the potentialities for attaining the
very highest in this respect in this life, so that we have no
right to despise any person whatever his station in life may
be.   The harbouring of racial and caste prejudice is moreover
detrimental to one's mental health and spiritual state and
it is a characteristic of the spiritually enlightened that they
shed them and act with love and impartiality towards all.
Race and caste discrimination are also inimical to social
progress since they bring about artificial and unreal divisions
among human beings where none exist and hinder harmonious relations.

The close analogy between racial and caste prejudice and
discrimination and the possible racial origin of much of the
latter has been referred to; although in essence 'caste prejudice is an aspect of culture prejudice, while race prejudice—as
distinguished from culture prejudice—is colour-and-physique
prejudice'.[1] In fact, even class prejudice within the same
'racial' group can have strong affinities with racial prejudice
so that the problems of race, caste and class cannot be divorced

---

[1] O. C. Cox, *Caste, Class and Race* (New York, 1948), p. 350.

from each other. The history of mercantilism shows how far an economic motive can form the basis for the exploitation of one class of people by another, even of a homogeneous racial group. As Cox points out, 'The mercantilist feared the prospects of the labourer's getting out of his place. It was felt that some class of people should be depended upon to do the common work, and that the status of this class as common workers should remain permanent. It was some tendency in the working class to be independent which called forth reactions akin to racial antagonism. Writing in 1770, William Temple says: "Our manufacturing populace have adopted a notion that as Englishmen they enjoy a birth right privilege of being more free and independent than any country in Europe. . . . The less the manufacturing poor have of it, the better for themselves and for the estate. The labouring people should never think of themselves as independent of their superiors for, if a proper subordination is not kept up, riot and confusion will take the place of sobriety and good order." That is, let us interpose, precisely the idea of 'the Negroes' place' in the United States.'[1] To keep them in their place they had to be denied the right to be educated. For, as Mandeville said in 1723: 'To make the society happy and people easy under the meanest circumstances, it is requisite that great numbers of them should be ignorant as well as poor.' Only a rationalization in the form of a race myth or a caste myth was needed in order to numb the consciences of the ruling classes and offer them an 'explanation' of their lot to the labouring classes. And such a rationalization would have been an easy affair when the downtrodden class was 'racially' different from the ruling class.

The Buddhist way of solving these problems is to seek for the causes and conditions which bring them about or accentuate them and then proceed to eradicate these causal factors. The Buddhist diagnosis would be that the causes are found in man as an individual as well as in society as an organization. According to Buddhism the springs of action of human individuals are greed, hatred, and delusion (or erroneous beliefs) as well as their opposites. The Buddhist view is that unless the former are entirely replaced by their opposites—charity, love and wisdom—man is in need of salvation and that in any case unless the former are toned

---

1. ibid., p. 340.

70

down no just society can be founded. The greed for economic and political power can be so great as to blind people to the nature, feelings and needs of individuals other than themselves or of human groups other than those they (erroneously) identify themselves with. Hatred can also find an easy outlet towards human beings or groups considered as alien or hostile to oneself or one's group. And as the Buddhist texts say greed and hatred nurture erroneous beliefs or delusions ('rationalizations') such as the racial and caste myths which we evolve out of our imagination with no basis in fact. These myths or erroneous beliefs in turn encourage our racial hatred and lust for power at the expense of our fellow men. Add to this the ignorance of the fact that we are prejudiced, as well as the costs of prejudice, and the process goes on within our minds, warping our personalities, shutting the door to spiritual experience and causing division and disharmony in human society. A change of heart and a change of outlook and attitude at the level of the individual is the solution to this problem. But such a transformation cannot be achieved by waiting for the operation of evolutionary processes or the grace of a divine being but only by putting forth effort on our own part. The erroneous beliefs that we entertain about race or caste have to be replaced by awareness of the facts before greed can give place to true charity and hatred to love.

But if a change of heart and outlook is essential on the part of individuals who harbour such prejudices it is equally important that a change in the organization of human society should be made. Buddhism conceives of society as a changing process subject to causal laws and it can change for better or worse. It is a popular misconception of Buddhism in the Western mind that it is only concerned about salvation and in the higher spiritual life and not in social reformation at all. The numerous sermons to laymen on the subject of their social well-being and the discourses on the nature of a righteous government and of a just society, coupled with the example of Asoka, leave no doubt that this aspect has received serious attention in Buddhism.

While the importance of the ideological factor as a social determinant is recognized—'the world is led by ideas or ideologies' (*cittena loko niyati*) it is significant that social evils as well as the growth of hatred in society are ultimately traced to the presence of poverty in human society or the maldistribution of economic goods. It is said in a *sutta*

sermon) which deals with the subject in an allegorical form
and a prophetic tone: 'Thus, brethren, as a result of the maldistribution of goods, poverty grows rife; from poverty grow-
ing rife stealing increases, from the spread of stealing violence
grows apace, from the growth of violence the destruction of
life becomes common... lying... evil speaking... adultery...
abusive and idle talk... covetousness and ill-will... false
opinions... incest, wanton greed and perverted lust... till
finally lack of filial and religious piety.... Among such
humans keen animosity will become the rule...'[1] The elimina-
tion of economic inequalities in human society will therefore
be an essential precondition for the emergence of harmonious
relations among human beings, so that what is required is both
a change of heart as well as a change of system.

Such sweeping changes can however only be brought about
by—as they are the responsibility of—those who at present
wield economic and political power in the world. The individual can only make decisions for himself and employ in
his own way the weapons of rational persuasion and example.

Except when truly Buddhist kings like Asoka were in
power, when political and legal methods were possible, these
were the weapons that the Sangha or the Order of Monks and
Nuns as well as lay Buddhist individuals employed. The
Sangha is the oldest historical institution which has had as
its members people of diverse races, castes, classes and tribes
who have shed their racial prejudices for the universalism of
the Order. In reflecting the Buddhist conception of the
equality of man its structure is democratic. As Mookerji
says, 'the Pali texts furnish interesting information of the
working of the Buddhist Samghas in strict and minute conform-
ity with genuine democratic principles'. [2] It is not controll-
ed by a pope or a hierarchy of ecclesiastics of any particular
nation. When new countries were converted the sons of the
soil took over very soon after, so that we do not find for
instance a Chinese Church of Japan or a Ceylonese Church
of Burma.

It is also noteworthy that there were no crusades in Buddhism, which never lent itself to imperial expansion and the
subjugation of peoples. There has been no military or political campaign or conquest with the idea of spreading Buddhist
culture and civilization.

---

1. Cakkavattisihanada Sutta, Digha Nikaya.
2. R. K. Mookerji, op. cit., p. 209,

72

The pacifism of Buddhism, as well as the absence of an 'out-group' feeling directed towards non-Buddhists on embracing Buddhism, is perhaps largely responsible for this, as is also the fact that the Dhamma is not considered a unique revelation which alone contains the sole truth. The Buddhist definition of 'the right philosophy of life' was comprehensive enough to contain, recognize and respect whatever truth other religions may have. According to the Buddhist conception of conversion, each person has to realize the truth for himself and rather than be hostile towards the ignorant one has to be compassionate and helpful towards them. The use of threats or force or the utilization of economic and social ncentives for conversion was evidently considered futile for such a purpose.